RECONCILING

RECONCILING

A LIFELONG STRUGGLE TO BELONG

LARRY GRANT

IN CONVERSATION WITH
SCOTT STEEDMAN

Published by ECW Press
665 Gerrard Street East
Toronto, Ontario, Canada M4M 1Y2
416-694-3348 / info@ecwpress.com

Editor for the Press: Jen Sookfong Lee
Copy editor: Carrie Gleason
Cover design: Jess Albert
Cover artwork: Jacyln (Adobe Stock) and Jess Albert

LIBRARY AND ARCHIVES CANADA CATALOGUING
IN PUBLICATION

Title: Reconciling : a lifelong struggle to belong /
Larry Grant ; in conversation with Scott Steedman.

Names: Grant, Larry (Musqueam Elder), author |
Steedman, Scott, author

Description: Includes bibliographical references.

Identifiers: Canadiana (print) 2025022397X |
Canadiana (ebook) 20250225352

ISBN 978-1-77041-798-4 (softcover)
ISBN 978-1-77852-483-7 (PDF)
ISBN 978-1-77852-482-0 (ePub)

Subjects: LCSH: Grant, Larry (Musqueam
Elder) | LCSH: Vancouver (B.C.)—Biography. |
CSH: Musqueam—Biography. | CSH: Chinese
Canadians—Biography. | CSH: First Nations—
Mixed descent. | LCGFT: Autobiographies.

Classification: LCC E99.S21 G73 2025 | DDC
971.1/330049794—dc23

This book is funded in part by the Government of Canada. *Ce livre est financé en partie par le gouvernement du Canada.* We acknowledge the support of the Canada Council for the Arts. *Nous remercions le Conseil des arts du Canada de son soutien.* We would like to acknowledge the funding support of the Ontario Arts Council (OAC) and the Government of Ontario for their support. We also acknowledge the support of the Government of Ontario through the Ontario Book Publishing Tax Credit, and through Ontario Creates.

PRINTED AND BOUND IN CANADA

PRINTING: MARQUIS   5 4 3 2 1

Get the
ebook free!*
*proof of purchase
required

Purchase the print edition and receive the ebook free.
For details, go to ecwpress.com/ebook.

To our mothers,
Agnes Grant and Jocelyn Steedman,
for making us who we are

θəʔit təθ qʷel

"Your words are true"

Contents

A Note on Orthography

For thousands of years, the Musqueam people have spoken hən̓q̓əmin̓əm̓, a Salishan language. In 1997, they chose to write hən̓q̓əmin̓əm̓ using the North American Phonetic Alphabet (NAPA) because, unlike the Latin alphabet used to spell English, it includes specialized symbols designed to encourage correct pronunciation.

As a hən̓q̓əmin̓əm̓ speaker and teacher and the Interim Manager of the Musqueam Language & Culture department at the Musqueam Indian Band, Larry Grant wanted to use NAPA spelling for hən̓q̓əmin̓əm̓ words in this book. To learn more about pronunciation, visit musqueam.bc.ca/departments/community-services /language/.

Introduction

People of the məθkʷəý Plant / At the Mouth of the Fraser River

"sʔəyələq is my name. I'm the son of θəwəχəlwət, Agnes Grant, and 洪禮興, Hong Tim Hing, and the grandson of Seymour Grant. My English name is Larry Grant."

Larry is a short, weathered man of eighty-five years with a calm, reassuring voice and piercing dark eyes hidden behind thick glasses. He's an Elder of both the Vancouver Chinese community and the Musqueam Indian Band, and he's standing on the muddy north bank of the north arm of staɬəw̓ (the Fraser River), on the edge of the village of xʷməθkʷəy̓əm, called by Canadian law "Musqueam Indian Reserve No. 2." It's late March 2022, and pandemic restrictions stopping non-Musqueam people from visiting the reserve have just been lifted. A southwest wind blows through the tall grasses by the riverbank as Larry talks, rippling the brown water of the Fraser and the dark blue of the Pacific Ocean off to the west, where the snow-tipped mountains of Vancouver Island shimmer diamond-hard on the horizon. A bald eagle soars high above his head and a flock of ducks shelter in the shade of a leafless poplar. It's a peaceful, calming spot—but one that's changed enormously in the span of Larry's lifetime.

"Vancouver is truly within Musqueam sacred territory," he says. He points north towards the heavily treed cliffs that obscure Marine Drive as he explains that his people used to catch fish—salmon, sturgeon, oolichan—and gather clams and mussels all along here, at the mouth of the river and along the shore of what is now Wreck Beach, below the main campus of the University of British Columbia (UBC). A century and a half of industry and development have transformed this beautiful, meditative land-scape; for millennia before contact, the river was shallow and slow-moving here, the artery of a green, flourishing marshland.

"Physically, the change has been astronomical," Larry says. His grandparents travelled by canoe or on foot; his grandmother told stories of walking to New Westminster, twenty-some kilometres to the east, along pathways following the river, to trade goods with the white merchants there. "Growing up, we had outhouses, we did not have electric lights, we did not have pavement. We didn't even have a gravel road, we had a dirt road. The one road that was used mostly was Crown Street," now a leafy suburban street lined with mansions and bungalows.

Larry grew up on the reserve in awe of his grandfather, Seymour Grant, a cultural authority, boat builder, logger and fisherman who was born around 1860—two years before the first Europeans settled in what is now the City of Vancouver. Seymour held one of the last great potlatches before they were banned, and gave permission for his daughter Agnes to marry Larry's father, a Chinese immigrant who had paid the Head Tax to enter Canada.

Larry has always thought that his mother, who was born in 1906 and raised on the reserve, lived in a fascinating time: "She went from a canoe to a horse and buggy to a Model T to an electric railroad. Then the airport was developed across the river from us. Little Piper Cubs flying up in the air. Pretty soon there were big airplanes coming in after the war. Then the Vampire jets come in, vroom vroom! Then the man on the moon—our mother's lifetime spanned all of that."

Vancouver's growth since his grandfather's time has been phenomenal. In 1871, the year British Columbia joined Canada, this logging town in a far-flung corner of the British Empire was home to less than a thousand settlers. Ten years later the province's total population was still less than fifty thousand people, half of them Indigenous. The Canadian Pacific Railway, finished in 1885 with the labour of seventeen thousand Chinese immigrants paid a dollar a day, launched a period of exponential development. A century and a half later Metro Vancouver is a multicultural metropolis of glass towers, tech start-ups and yoga studios with a population of three million. Seymour Grant would barely recognize his home at the mouth of the Fraser River.

///////////

It's taken most of Larry's long life for his extraordinary cultural heritage to be appreciated. He has lived on the reserve, in a house he built for himself, since 1985, when he and his siblings finally won a thirty-four-year legal battle to be recognized as status members of the Musqueam Nation. The story of that battle, and why they had to fight it, spans more than a century, from the day in 1920 when Larry's father left his family village of Sei Moon in Guangdong, China, and got on a steamer bound for Vancouver and a farm at the mouth of the Fraser River.

"When we were kids, we used to watch them dredging that river all the time, so that the tugboats and barges could go upriver,"

Larry says, pointing at the muddy water rushing past on the ebbing tide. "The big ships would go up the main arm at Steveston. They gradually built the jetty that's out there today. It wasn't that length when we were kids and didn't exist at all when my mother was growing up in the early 1900s." The North Arm Jetty, a slender, sandy, human-made breakwater begun in 1916 and now 6.8 kilometres long, encouraged the river to self-scour, to keep the channel narrow and deep enough to stop sand from settling in the riverbed.

Thanks to all that scouring, the river mouth is busy with maritime traffic today: tugboats pulling log booms, fishing boats heading for the Strait of Georgia, yachts on pleasure cruises, lumbering barges heavy with wood chips, whale-watching boats taking tourists in search of orcas. Jet and float planes land and take off at Vancouver International Airport, whose air traffic control tower scans the skies to the south. The sun ripples off the log booms that bob in the dark-blue sea as far as the eye can see west and north, on the vast booming grounds between the jetty and the shore.

When Larry was a boy, the far bank of the river was just sand and sheet piling—wooden poles driven into the shoreline to guide the river in its course. "They gradually backfilled it, when Iona Spit was made," he says. The reclaimed land increased the size of Iona Island, the land across the river from the reserve, which now houses a sewage plant, an animal refuge and a park popular with birders because of the rare species that stop here on their way to and from migrating grounds in the Arctic. And it's no longer an island; it's since been joined to Sea Island, the home of the airport, by a causeway.

Larry laughs at the name "Iona," after the Scottish island that was home to a famous medieval monastery and now hosts spiritual retreats. Who would put a sewage treatment plant on holy ground? "The Sacred Island of Shit, we kids called it," he says with a chuckle.

The reserve sits at the western tip of the delta of one of North America's great rivers. staɬəw̓ (the Fraser River) starts in the northern Rocky Mountains on the border with Alberta and carries fertile glacial silt from a wide swathe of British Columbia on its 1,400-kilometre journey to the Pacific Ocean, which ends just a few metres west of where Larry is standing. When he was growing up, the river flowed through a lush, near-pristine estuary ecosystem, though industry was beginning to make its mark. The channel was still wide and shallow then, meandering through tranquil wetlands abounding with fish and water birds. In his diary, explorer Simon Fraser called the waterway that now bears his name "a small winding river."

"Our history says our people have been here forever; the archaeologists say thousands and thousands of years," Larry says. "We've always lived at the mouth of the river, beginning at Hope and moving downwards as the delta was being formed. The ice age ended ten to fifteen thousand years ago. On the south side of the Alex Fraser Bridge, archaeological evidence is carbon-dated back six thousand years. That was səw̓q̓ʷeqsən, a huge village site." It sits twenty kilometres upriver from the sea today, on the south side of a concrete bridge surrounded by sawmills and warehouses.

"The diversity of the marsh system was a lot richer than it is today," Larry adds, pointing north towards the dayglow green of Shaughnessy Golf and Country Club and the neighbourhood suburbs beyond. "The grasses, ducks, all the sea life then. There were a lot of muskrats along the foreshore and up the river, for instance;

in our childhood people were still trapping them. Now they're gone. The fur trading companies, the Hudson's Bay, would buy the fur."

The steady growth of Vancouver and the farms of the Fraser Valley over the last century has transformed the river, and the reserve at its mouth. "All of the pollution that was created by developing communities, the agriculture, the ranching, and all those toxic chemicals that were not regulated at that time—they polluted the whole foreshore, all the way down the river for miles, from the Coquitlam area."

Larry says the dirty beachfront we are standing on was once all white from clam shells. "Right off what's now called Point Grey was a clam bed, and mussels too. It's documented by Fisheries. A few years after colonization, settlers fished it all out." Further upriver, from Marpole and above, a creosote plant and agricultural waste polluted the waters until what shellfish survived were no longer edible. "You can still see it in False Creek," Larry says. "The mussels on the pilings are creosoted, contaminated, toxic."

As a kid he remembers seeing them and asking his mum, "Why can't we eat those?"

"Because they're poisoned," she answered.

"There's still a herring run in False Creek, but it's tiny compared to what it was," Larry adds. "And the warming of the water is threatening the salmon too. Now California sea lions are moving north. You can see them in False Creek."

⁂

Larry was born in 1936, in an outhouse in a farmer's field near the tiny town of Agassiz, at the eastern end of the Fraser Delta. Like many Indigenous people back then, his family was reduced to relying on seasonal work, in this case picking hops for a local company; after the harvest was over, his mother returned to her father's house on the reserve and took care of her newborn son there.

"My first memory of being here is around three years of age," Larry recalls. "The language that was spoken to me then was hən̓q̓əmin̓əm̓"—the Musqueam language, the "downriver" dialect of Halkomelem, a Salishan language—"and a little bit of English. And my father spoke Cantonese to me."

"My mum spoke good English, without an accent," Larry recalls. "We kids chose to be Canadian, that's why we concentrated on learning English, not Cantonese or hən̓q̓əmin̓əm̓," his mother's tongue.

When they were kids, Larry and his siblings were free to walk anywhere. Back then, before the golf course swallowed up almost half the reserve land, the riverbank where he is standing was lower and the marshes spread for hundreds of metres to the north and west, a wonderful playground of head-high grasses concealing little creeks and ditches and mud and every kind of bug and beast. "There were sinkholes all over," he recalls with a laugh. "You had to watch your step or you would sink in right up to your neck!"

The word *Musqueam* refers to a flowering plant, probably a tall flowering lily, from the Fraser estuary—the literal translation is *People of the məθkʷəy̓ plant*. "We're not too sure what məθkʷəy̓ is," Larry explains. "Our grandparents said when we were kids that they had not actually seen it but had heard the descriptions of it. But they are conflicting descriptions, or maybe just variations. We're not sure exactly which plant it is."

When they were playing in the marshes, Larry and his brothers and sister were haunted by the story of sʔi:ɬqəy̓, a double-headed snake that was said to live in a small lake called xʷməṁqʷe:m (Camosun Bog, a protected wetland of rare plants near what is now 16th Avenue and Crown Street). The old people warned them to be wary of this monstrous serpent and stay away from its watery lair. The great reptile was said to be so thick and heavy that when it slithered from the lake to staɬəẃ (the Fraser River) it ground out the bed of stélqəy (Tin Can Creek, the little waterway that still flows through Musqueam today). Everything the serpent touched died, and from its droppings bloomed a new plant, the məθkʷəẏ, which gave its name to both the place and the people who lived there.

There were real snakes out there in the marshes; not just little garter snakes but bigger bull snakes, thick black creatures that lay in wait in the reeds. They ate rodents, such as rats and mice. "We'd be wading out there and it'd be, holy smokes, there's a snake there!" Larry says. "They were long—sixty centimetres to a metre," he says, stretching out his hands like an excited angler. "They looked like giant snakes to us, but we were small then. Bigger than garter snakes, anyway."

Larry and his friends also used to play on the *mali*, the hən̓q̓əmin̓əm̓ name for the east end of Wreck Beach. The tidal flats there were overgrown with bullrushes and sedge grasses, a wonderful world to explore when the tide was out. "The whole foreshore there was a booming ground," says Larry, "a tie-up area for log booms. We would go along the beach and play on the booms, although we weren't supposed to, and see what we could find. Prior to them putting up the jetty, there were many boats and scows wrecked on the shore there—that's how it gets its name, Wreck Beach."

//////////////

People forget how isolated the reserve used to be, Larry says. "You came down Crown Street, there was nothing—one house! I remember a big sign on a gate there: 'Nell Grove lives here.' All the other houses you see there now didn't exist."

"My mother was a fluent speaker of hənq̓əmin̓əm̓," Larry says. "She was one of the last really fluent speakers—people came to her to ask the names of animals and plants and things like that. But we didn't speak much hənq̓əmin̓əm̓ as children. When I was growing up, I heard the Vancouver Island dialect a lot. Many of our families have relatives over on Vancouver Island."

He also has family who have been on the North Shore for many generations, in what is now West and North Vancouver. In Musqueam oral history, that side of Burrard Inlet was also hənq̓əmin̓əm̓-speaking territory. The original territory in their specific use area—which was designated in the 1970s by over seventy Musqueam Elders—ranged from sʔəlqsən (Point Grey) to the Harvey Creek area near present-day Lions Bay, at the mouth of Howe Sound. It also reached over the mountains and down səlilwətaʔɬ (Indian Arm) into Port Moody, xʷmiṁsəcsəṁ (Coquitlam) and q̓ic̓əy̓ (Katzie, near Maple Ridge), then up into q̓ʷənɬən (Kwantlen) and back down the south side to scəw̓aθən (Tsawwassen) and back to the north side of the Fraser. Musqueam Reserve No. 2 is just under two hundred hectares, one-fifth of 1 percent of the Musqueam's traditional territory.

"Pre-contact, before Europeans came, all that was the Musqueam language area," Larry says. "And that does not include our secondary-use area. Our community used to go all the way up into the Fraser Canyon harvesting fish, and down south to the Point Roberts area and up into the mountain ranges in our hunting and gathering; getting wool from mountain goats for weaving, picking berries and a lot of roots and things that were used at that time. So that did not include those secondary-use territories. Today it seems that we have a small area of claim, but it doesn't include that secondary-use area."

For Larry, the real connection to all this land is the hənq̓əmińəm̓ language. Every little nook and cranny has a hənq̓əmińəm̓ name from before contact. "Our connection is between the language and the land, and all the resources on the land and in the water, the trees and the animals. We had names for all of these things prior to contact."

"It's hard to say," Larry replies when asked about the size of the Musqueam Nation pre-contact. "Numbers run between thirty-five thousand and sixty-five thousand people in the inlet area. You can't just think of the reserve today, there were a multitude of communities throughout the area."

All this talk of water and creeks has led Larry a couple of hundred metres upstream, where an ugly concrete block sticks out into the river. "This is our slough," he says with a shake of the head. "Part of one of the creeks that come down to the river. We're standing on top of a shitty tunnel, literally—a pipe that goes through our lands and up to Dunbar," a fancy neighbourhood south of even fancier Point Grey. "The Highbury Tunnel they call it. The land it uses was expropriated from our reserve by the GVRD [Greater Vancouver Regional District] all the way up to Marine Drive, back when they were allowed to do that sort of thing without consultation." It is still in use, carrying sewage from the posh West Side through the reserve and under the river to the treatment plant on Iona Island.

Just upstream is a little bay where a log and a Coke can are bobbing in an eddy. "Back in the day, our grandfathers tied up their boats here," Larry explains. "Sometimes they needed to paint the bottoms, do repairs, so they brought them up on the banks here. They'd even leave them for the winter. Though usually they would tie them up at Celtic, the BC Packers shipyard, if they could afford it."

The area around the reserve saw the first contacts between the Coast Salish people, the original residents of present-day Vancouver, and European mariners. In the late 1700s, the warrior chief qiyəplenəxʷ (Capilano), Larry's great-great-grandfather, lived in a fortified site on the beach just north of where he is now standing, with the families of other warriors, mostly Musqueam. They fought battles in the area, and greeted the first Spanish and British explorers, including José María Narváez (in 1791) and Captain George Vancouver (1792), from the high cliffs above the beach, which have sweeping views across the strait to Vancouver Island. (Captain Vancouver sailed past Wreck Beach and north into Burrard Inlet on July 13, 1792, having somehow managed to *not* notice either of the mouths of the huge river to the south, one of the main aims of his expedition.)

"This here is probably where Simon Fraser arrived, as close as he got to the sea," Larry adds, pointing to the spot where his grandfathers moored their canoes. "He pulled his canoe in here, used to be a tidal bay."

The American-born Scottish-Canadian explorer Fraser descended the river that now bears his name in July 1808, the first white person to do so. He was in the final stage of a journey of discovery for the fur traders of the North West Company, who were trying to establish a route to the sea. The First Nations Fraser met as he canoed and hiked down the canyon were friendly at first, but they turned on him when he "borrowed" a canoe without permission early one morning. His crew of twenty-four had just escaped the treacherous canyon around Hell's Gate and reached the calm delta, so they raced for the ocean, but word of their "borrowing" reached the Musqueam before they did, and they sent out a war party to stop him. Fraser and his men had to paddle back up the river as fast as their arms could power them. They saw the Pacific Ocean but never reached it, which makes Larry chuckle.

"That's Simon Fraser's lookout," he says, pointing north to a viewpoint on Marine Drive that overlooks the reserve and the river mouth. "We have the plaque that used to be there; it quotes Simon Fraser's diary about how he was stopped by a group of Musqueam warriors, who 'began to make their appearance from every direction howling like so many wolves, and brandishing their war clubs.' That's how they used to talk back then."

For the first time in three years, canoe racing is going ahead on the river this spring, although the people on the reserve are still wary of covid. Each weekend for six weeks, a different Coast Salish community in BC, Washington or Oregon will host a race. The Musqueam race is set for May 24, and the canoes will launch here, in Simon Fraser's eddy. "You go down that ramp and just walk it into the river," explains Larry. "It's shallow for a fair bit, so you can put the bow in and swing it around."

The other races will be held up and down the Fraser Valley, with the final one at Ambleside in West Vancouver. Anyone is welcome to come and watch. "It's good to see what they do with a canoe," says Larry. But mostly it's a good reason to visit relatives. "Everyone wants to just move and visit."

Larry's life echoes the barely known story of Vancouver—and most cities in the Americas and Oceania, from the Inca capital Cusco to Mexico City (the Aztecs' Tenochtitlan), from Manhattan ("the place where bows are found" in the Algonquian language Lenape) to Sydney, from Honolulu (Polynesian for "sheltered harbour") to Wellington to Toronto (Mohawk for "where there are trees standing in water"). Except in Vancouver, colonization is astonishingly recent, despite many Vancouverites' total amnesia towards their own history. Within living memory, or just about; Larry remembers his grandparents very well, and they were born before English was more than a whisper in the spectacular landscape that now hosts Western Canada's largest city. Four generations or 160 years ago, the only words spoken here were in həṅq̓əmiṅəm̓ and other Salishean languages, the native tongues of the Salish Sea area. Talking to Larry or any other Indigenous Elder is a way of communing with pre-contact British Columbia.

Larry's life also combines ancient Indigenous traditions with key events in the last two centuries, including Chinese immigration and the Head Tax; the ravages of residential school, only now being properly recognized; the misogyny and ongoing paternalism of the Indian Act, still the legal basis for most government-Indigenous relations in Canada; the "Potlatch Ban" on Indigenous art, spirituality and ceremony, which forced the Musqueam to relinquish or hide their traditional beliefs for close to a century; and now reconciliation and Indigenous revival and an accompanying change in worldview.

This change includes attitudes to the environment. Other than Wreck Beach and the marshes by the river mouth, the area around the reserve was mostly rainforest a century ago, dark glades of massive coniferous trees two and three metres wide and thirty to forty high. "All of Metro Vancouver was mostly rainforest," Larry says. "Metro Vancouver today is the largest clear-cut in the southwest corner of the province. You have to think about it that way. Even Stanley Park is second and third growth. There was a Musqueam village by the Deadman Island side, and another village on Prospect Point that was part of our community. And another one at Point Atkinson, by Lighthouse Park [in West Vancouver].

"There was also a big village at Locarno Beach, close to UBC. That is a huge, huge village site, part of the Jericho–Locarno Beach area. Many of the homes that are built on the side hill and along the shoreline there have disrupted the burial sites and middens of that community. It was quite a large community, it's called ʔəy̓alməxʷ. That whole area was populated prior to contact."

Larry reminds us that like Stanley Park, the entire stunning beachscape of Spanish Banks, Locarno and Jericho beaches, one of the jewels of the city, is an artificial creation of the twentieth century. The sand where swimsuit-clad visitors sunbathe and play volleyball was shipped in, as were the neatly trimmed logs bathers love to lounge on. At contact this was a village site by a lush marsh, fed by small streams and alive with fish, birds and people like the mouth of the Fraser, where the reserve is now.

Most of the streams that once flowed through Point Grey have been pushed underground, through culverts. "Those were salmon-bearing streams. With the salmon being around, that attracts all that wildlife that eats salmon. They've been closed over. Across Metro Vancouver, from here to Coquitlam at least, they covered over about fifty streams, the majority of which were salmon-bearing. It's the real estate guys making millions on unceded land.

"Also, I don't know if you've been around salmon streams at the time of spawning; it gets pretty high, and the new society ladies coming over didn't like that. It wasn't attractive, that smell, the smell of life and death, the dying fish, the rotting flesh. So that's all part of that."

⁂

Just then a Musqueam Council administrator, out for a walk on her break, stops to say hi to Larry. They talk for a bit about last night's Zoom meeting, about what to do with some extra funds that have come in because of a ruling increasing rents on band territory.

"What I said at the meeting was, we are not well!" says Larry. "We have to deal with that first. You look at all the problems, drugs, alcohol—we don't have a choice, we have to get well first. I've heard that over and over—from MCC [Musqueam Capital Corporation], from my aunties. Try to say that without raising hackles! It's just what I feel. I'm just laying my cards on the table. You disagree, I get defensive too—we have to stop and think."

He explains that the discussions about how to spend the money can get heated. "Some people say, we've been poor all our lives, now it's time to enjoy ourselves, I'd like to buy a new truck. OK, but for me, it's over. I'm thinking long term, about my grandchildren"—he flattens the palm of his hand at hip height— "they're the people we have to look out for. We live in poverty, financially, though we are well-off in services. Not as good as the surrounding community though."

He goes on to say that these days he gets asked to do land acknowledgments all the time, often at conferences or other events at UBC. He always stays a while afterwards and listens to the keynote speakers. "You learn a lot," he says. "That's why I encourage all the young people to do that too."

His whole worldview was shaken up at a conference a few years ago on early childhood education, when he heard UBC psychiatry professor Adele Diamond talking about childhood trauma. "She said that exclusion is as damaging, does as much harm to the child's development, as drugs or alcohol. I heard that, and it really stuck with me. That was a really high moment for me, holy cow." For Larry, the whole Musqueam community suffers from the trauma of exclusion, a residue of residential school—which he was fortunate to avoid.

He's now standing next to a beautiful wooden shed decorated with bright bas-reliefs. "That's our canoe carving shed," he explains. "Some band members who are UBC psychology students got a grant for that. They've now carved three fifty-foot canoes in it. It's like a rebirth; it was decades since the last canoes had been carved."

A tugboat churns by, pushing big waves into the line of piles that snakes seaward and past it onto the shore. "There used to be booms tied up to those piles," Larry says. "There aren't so many loose logs now."

"This land we're on now is all infill," he explains, pointing to the reedy mudflats to the north. "We raised it up. That's where the level used to be. This here was all six feet under. We got into a big fight with the North Fraser Harbour Commission about it. They say the process has to be natural accretion, you can't just fill it in. That was 1985, and we've been arguing about it ever since. We say it contravenes the original reserve document:

'These Indians can reclaim land on tidal flats.' We're still fighting with the GVRD over it."

He almost steps on the bloody remains of several ducks; severed feet and heads, wings, entrails. "Don't harass an eagle!" he says with a chuckle.

A few hundred metres inland stands the Big House, an imposing wooden structure that looks like a barn from afar. It rises to a peak, with two wide, rectangular chimneys like skylights puffing smoke into the grey March sky. Two band members come out of a back door and light up cigarettes in the shade of a poplar. Someone is being initiated, Larry explains. A member of the Masked Dance Society himself, Larry has participated in traditional Musqueam ceremonies here for three-quarters of a century, since 1946: marriages, ancestral namings, initiations, female puberty rites, winter and summer dances.

A lot of band members are uncomfortable with the traditional ways, Larry explains. Many of them are Christian, and they worry that the old beliefs are blasphemous. He respects that, but has never had any problem with the old belief system of his mother and her parents.

∕∕∕∕∕∕∕∕∕∕∕∕∕

Musqueam Indian Reserve No. 2 is one of Canada's few urban Indian reserves, home to 1,766 people, who live on an area just under two square kilometres. Larry points out that the Musqueam have less land per capita than any other Indigenous Nation in Canada. "My whole life it's been, 'You Indians get stuff for free.' Hell: this is our land, you never paid us a penny for it. *You're* getting it free.

"That's what I told Christy Clark, when she was premier: 'I see the province has a land transfer tax, just give us that!'"

When Larry talks about reconciliation, he uses the verb: *reconciling*, a process we're all going through, Indigenous and settler, immigrant and Canadian-born. "I have been reconciling my whole life, with my inner self," he explains. "With being part Chinese, part Musqueam, status, non-status, then status again. Growing up not really being one or the other. And all that without my consultation, without my free, informed, prior consent. To not belong was forced upon me by the colonial society that surrounded me. But reconciling with myself is part of all that. Though I didn't have a choice—I didn't ask to be excluded from all that stuff."

His wife tells him that when he talks about these things, he gets fired up; his voice starts to rise. "So it's still in there, the trauma, the hurt, the rejection, I'm still living with that. Until you come to reconciliation with yourself, you can't think logically."

Larry adds that he now realizes he can't help being half Musqueam and half Chinese. "I've got to the point where every day I thank my father for coming all this way, and for meeting my mother. 'Even though you were a foreigner in my country—I'm half of that too!' It's taken me years to accept that, to be able to say it out loud. If you can't do that, you can't reconcile.

"And once you've sorted that out, it's a lifelong journey to maintain it, without judging. Then you can help others."

At which point Larry goes quiet, standing on the grey beach by the river with the salty estuarine wind in his lined face. Small waves from a passing barge ripple onto the shore and he steps lightly aside to keep his shoes dry. High overhead the eagle, soaring effortlessly all this time, swoops suddenly and banks over the poplars, where the ducks still cower in the shadows. Larry smiles, turns his back on the water and heads up towards his office.

Chapter One

Born in an Outhouse /
At the Top of the Fraser Valley

Today, on a cold but sunny February afternoon, it's all corn fields, muddy and fallow. A biting wind is swirling dust into little tornado plumes in the moist riverside air. Larry is walking along the verge of Whelpton Road in Agassiz, a tiny farming community 130 kilometres due east of Musqueam Indian Reserve No. 2 at the top of the Fraser Delta, looking for the place where he was born. Flat fields stretch away in all directions, their green stubble scarred by tractor tracks, hemmed in by the looming bulk of the Coast Mountains to the north, east and south, sparkling with fresh snow in the icy winter sunshine.

"I wasn't expecting this," Larry says. He looks around, zipping up his coat and trying to imagine his family here eighty-six years ago. "What's the address again?"

"Whelpton Road, Agassiz. No number."

In the distance he spies a slowly collapsing white barn and a few shacks hidden by silhouetted, windblown poplars. A bald eagle soars past on the crisp winter air. "I can see this ain't a hops field," Larry says. "Things come and go, there's no trace of it anymore."

He was born in 1936 in one of these fields, in an outhouse near a cabin owned by Hamersley's Hopyard, in the quiet stillness of a late summer's night. Like many Indigenous people back then, his mother's family had travelled up the Fraser Delta to pick hops, working long days in these same fields. He came into the world unexpectedly, long before his due date, the second of four siblings, at around midnight; he was never sure if his birthday was August 31 or September 1.

At the time, Hamersley's and a handful of smaller farms had turned Agassiz into one of the top hop-producing regions in the country, with about four hundred acres planted with hops vines. After harvesting, the plants' green, cone-shaped flowers were shipped to brewers across Canada and as far as the UK to add bitterness, stability and flavour to beer. From late August into October, when the plants bloomed, an army of itinerant workers came to Agassiz to pick the flowers from the plants by hand. At the industry's peak, it employed more than a thousand pickers, local farmers of European descent toiling alongside Chinese, Japanese and Mennonite workers. But the biggest single group was First Nations people, mostly Coast Salish from up and down the Fraser Valley and as far away as Vancouver Island, Washington state and the Okanagan Valley, who gathered here to make two or three dollars a day picking hops in the verdant fields by the Fraser River, their traditional lands.

Larry's mother and aunts told him later what hard work it was. "You bend over all the time, picking from the vines, off the ground. You have to stoop because you're picking it into a cloth bin, about a metre square. Might be two people working all along it," he says, gesturing with his hands to show how the hop vines are held up on strings. "It's tough on the back, and the hands. Nobody had gloves."

Seasonal agricultural work like this has always been the lot of the poorest of the poor, as it still is today. "They need slave labour," says Larry. "Who'll pick your berries? Your fruit? Your hops?"

The men had gone salmon fishing by late August, so the family group was comprised of old people, women and children: Larry's grandparents, aunts and older cousins. "They picked hops or berries to make money," Larry says, "but also to reconnect with other families, and to be able to support their kids in the summertime, if you didn't go and work in a cannery somewhere. Those were the only jobs they were able to get."

All the First Nations people would gather in the evenings and on Sundays for huge, inter-nation competitions like the ones at the Seabird Island Festival now held just upstream every May. The various nations would play baseball and soccer as well as hybrid Indigenous sports like dry canoe races (running with logs under their arms) and traditional Coast Salish wrestling. In the evenings there were salmon barbecues and singing and drumming around the campfires.

/////////////

A sign at the end of the road points towards a B&B, with "Closed" written across it. At the end of the road is another sign that reads, "Private drive, dogs on duty, no exit." It's bitterly cold, so Larry decides he's seen enough and suggests we head to town for lunch.

"This is uptown Agassiz," he says with a chuckle, surveying the tiny town centre. There are two Chinese restaurants, but Hong's Garden—his father's surname, and a surname Larry went by for many years—is closed, so we settle on a coffee shop that makes surprisingly good sandwiches.

During hop-picking time, many of the workers had to sleep in tents, but the year Larry was born his family was lucky to be put in a cabin. "They called it a cabin, but it was a shack," he says. "I don't think it was bigger than ten by twelve [feet], with bunks in it. Mum had her sisters with her, the whole family went up in the summertime. Dad was off working in Chinatown or on the farm."

During the night of August 31, his mum woke up with what felt like gas but turned out to be labour pains. It was far too early, so she wasn't sure and told her sister, "If I don't come back right away, come and get me—I'm going to the bathroom." Then she headed to the outhouse and had the baby there, quietly and all alone.

"I say that's why I have a crappy outlook on life—I was born in an outhouse," Larry deadpans. "I was born in the middle of the night, without any real lights. There were no lights in those places. My aunt heard me crying, woke up and went out, and I'd been born. Prematurely."

Very prematurely. Larry was so premature—two to three months—that the family wrapped him up in newspaper to keep him warm. "That's all they had. Because they weren't really expecting me. I was very small, I could fit in a shoebox. I guess Mum was either measuring me, in case I died, to know what size of a coffin to have—'He'll fit in a shoebox!'—or just making do." He puts his hands close together, like an actor on the stage. He's trying to be serious, but then his mouth bursts into a smile. He's told the story of his birth many times.

Larry's grandfather was worried the tiny baby boy wouldn't survive, so he told his daughter to do nothing else but look after her newborn. "She didn't have to go picking hops, just stayed in the cabin," Larry says. His skull hadn't solidified yet, so she had to keep rotating his head, so the brain case would not flatten.

By the time hop season was over a few weeks later, Larry's skull had finally solidified and he had outgrown the shoebox. So his mother returned to her father's house on the reserve and took care of her newborn son there.

A family picture shows Larry smiling in between one of his aunts and his mother, on the back of a truck. The women are still and perfectly in focus, but teenage Larry is a blur of motion. The family was going hop picking again, this time to Sardis, by Chilliwack and the Five Corners, twenty-five kilometres southeast of Agassiz.

"You know Chilliwack Mall? That used to be a hop field, by the old highway. One side of the highway became Chilliwack Mall, on the other side there's hotels there now. There was a drive-in theatre there for a while, until it shut down."

In 1948, twelve years after Larry's birth, Agassiz was overwhelmed by a massive flood that destroyed the entire hops crop. The town switched to growing corn, soon becoming the corn capital of BC. The Agassiz corn fields were submerged by severe flooding in 2021 when the Fraser burst its banks again.

The craft beer movement has led to a recent revival in hops production in the Fraser Valley. Bredenhof Hop Farms in neighbouring Abbotsford, founded in 2015, is now the biggest Canadian distributor of the flowers, which it sells to more than three hundred beer makers, from hipster microbreweries off Vancouver's Main Street to Molson Coors, a multinational with $11.7 billion in sales in 2023.

The reserve where Larry's parents met was a peaceful place largely free of the systemic racism that ruled the rest of Vancouver society in the 1920s and '30s. Since contact in 1791, the Musqueam had been devastated by European diseases: measles, tuberculosis, typhoid fever and, worst of all, smallpox, which tore through Indigenous communities from Washington state to Alaska in 1862, killing about two-thirds of the already-plummeting population in a single summer. From a population of about fifty thousand pre-contact, Musqueam band membership had slumped to only ninety-two people in 1900 but was slowly rebounding by the time Larry's parents got together in 1933; by Vancouver's fifty-year Golden Jubilee in 1936, it had gone past 160 (it's now eleven times that: 1,766).

In this as in many aspects of life, the Musqueam were subject to an accelerated version of the same brutal process that had decimated the Americas' Indigenous people since contact. Estimates vary, but there were probably sixty million people living here when Columbus stepped onto the white sands of the island of Guanahani in 1492 and promptly renamed it San Salvador. A hundred years later this number had plummeted to six million, meaning 90 percent of the population had died; in war and massacre, but also from smallpox and measles, and from slaving in the mines and plantations.

Under the Indian Act and the Reserve Act, Musqueam people were confined to their miniscule reserve, where their lives were managed by the "Indian agent," a federal bureaucrat based in New Westminster who oversaw dozens of Nations up and down the BC coast and on Vancouver Island and only visited the reserve once a month at most. He (they were all men) kept close tabs on his "wards," tracking people's movements and threatening them with removal of their Indian "status" if they strayed too far from the reserve. (One family, Ed Sparrow's, was warned to return immediately from a work trip to the Fraser Valley or they'd lose their band membership.)

From the 1830s to 1960s, Indian agents implemented federal policy on reserves and were responsible for keeping the government informed of all activity there. These tinpot dictators ruled the lives of Canada's Indigenous population, enforcing restrictions large and petty. They managed band finances and had to approve any economic activity like cutting down trees and selling the lumber, charging a fee and holding the money in trust. They also stripped women who married non-Indigenous men of their status and forced them to leave the reserve. (All this ended in the 1960s, when the role was phased out and new Indigenous governments began controlling their own affairs, including finances.)

Faced with all these restrictions, the Musqueam were cut off socially, geographically and economically. Hemmed in on their reserve, they had almost no interactions with the wealthy suburbs or vibrant city growing at breakneck speed all around them. "The reserve was a minimum-security prison," says Larry.

The Chinese faced a whole slew of different barriers. The first wave of Chinese immigrants came to British Columbia during the Fraser Gold Rush of 1858, creating vibrant Chinatowns in Victoria and Vancouver and smaller communities up the river in Hope, Quesnel and beyond. About seventeen thousand more came between 1881 and 1885, hired as cut-price labour to build the transcontinental railroad; it was dangerous, poorly paid work, and about six hundred are thought to have died from explosions and rock slides.

On July 20, 1885, three months before the last spike was hammered into the ground near Revelstoke, BC, the federal government began charging a fifty-dollar fee to discourage new arrivals from China. By 1903 this "Head Tax" had been increased to five hundred dollars, two years' salary for most workers. It was dropped in 1923, but only because all Chinese immigration was halted then until the so-called "Chinese Exclusion Act" was repealed in 1947. The total amount Chinese immigrants paid in "Head Taxes" is estimated at almost $23 million ($393 million in 2023 dollars)—only $2 million less than the federal government paid the Canadian Pacific Railway company to build the train line across the country.

The new arrivals then faced a labyrinth of other discriminatory policies. They could not vote or own Crown land, which was a particular stumbling block for farmers like Larry's grandfather, who arrived from a small rural village in China sometime around 1906 and was soon followed by his half-brothers and sons; one of the latter would become Larry's father.

"That's how the Musqueam and the Chinese became intertwined," Larry explains. "Indigenous people were denied integration within the surrounding community, and the Chinese were denied citizenship, denied access to a lot of land. Both were denied access to the professions, so they couldn't be lawyers, doctors, engineers. We couldn't be accepted into the life that surrounded us. Indigenous people were also denied access to post-secondary education, unless you went into theology and promoting the word of God." He rolls his eyes at that thought.

The Indian agent wanted the Musqueam, who had sustained themselves with fishing, hunting and gathering for millennia, to adapt to Canadian ways by becoming farmers. So these two marginalized groups—one with a background in farming but no land, the other with land but no tradition or desire to farm it—found one another.

"The Department of Indian Affairs were trying to make farmers out of the Aboriginal people, to be self-sustaining," Larry says. "However, we didn't come from an agricultural society as such—we were more 'aquacultural' people. And the Chinese garden farmers were the only people at that time allowed to lease property on the Indian reserve." The Indian agent got around the restriction on leasing farms on reserves by calling them "gardens" and the Chinese "gardeners."

"Those two denied groups supported each other in many endeavours," says Larry. "Because many Chinese businesses were not able to hire white people, or white women, they employed Indigenous women. Our grandfathers and grandmothers, and great-grandfathers and great-grandmothers, were accepting of other ethnic groups, unlike the white, British society that was coming in, full of denial of other people, other ethnic groups that were not white. And that's basically where my dad met my mother."

Chinese farmers had probably been leasing land from the Musqueam for years beforehand, but in 1909 the Indian agent made the arrangement official—with all money passing through him, naturally. By 1917, at least eighteen Chinese families were leasing small plots of Musqueam land. Larry's grandfather formed a sort of co-op company with his brothers and cousins and leased a ten-acre patch at what is now Salish Drive and 51st Street. Called Lin On Yuen (farm), it gradually grew to thirteen acres, with a wooden farmhouse where the men slept and ate. They worked long hours cultivating Chinese vegetables—bok choy, gai choy, gai lan—as well as lettuce, turnips, green onions and peas. The men supplied wholesalers and stores in Vancouver with produce, and later opened their own store in Chinatown.

"When they came from China and farmed here, our family, and all the other families, really did a big service for the community, and also the community of Vancouver," says Larry. "Supplying produce for the city, so many people are not aware of that—and it was right here in Musqueam."

///////////////

So it was that a young man by the name of Hong Tim Hing, later to become Larry's father, left China for Canada, the land of opportunity the Chinese called "Gold Mountain." At the age of fourteen, Tim Hing walked out of the farming village of Sei Moon, the family's ancestral home in the rich Pearl River Delta in Guangdong, then as now China's most populous province, and made his way east to the British colony of Hong Kong. On June 3, 1920, he boarded the steamship *Empress of Asia*, following in the footsteps of his father and several uncles who had made the same journey in the decades before. Like most of the other 1,200 passengers on board, he was in third class, in a small cabin below the waterline.

The Chung Collection at the University of British Columbia includes a scale model of the *Empress of Asia*, built like the original ship by the Canadian Pacific Steamship Company in Glasgow in 1912–13. With its polished wood, brass and wrought iron fittings, white top deck and dark red hull, it's a sleek and romantic vessel, with three large smokestacks, two tall wooden masts and four propellers that allowed it to set speed records in its early years. Like the later CPR steamship *Empress of Canada*, it spent the first decades of its life ferrying immigrants from Japan, China and Hong Kong to Vancouver, its home port—a kind of feeder for the CPR's transcontinental railroad.

Larry likes to imagine his father looking out the porthole of his tiny cabin—passengers in steerage weren't allowed on deck— as the massive ship set sail for Canada, the greatest adventure of his life truly begun. He wonders what was going through the teenager's mind, travelling alone with false papers and, quite possibly, a hidden wad of cash; some Chinese immigrants sewed money into secret compartments in their clothes. "Although he wasn't allowed in first class, the food was actually better in third class," Larry says. "Our father could order any Chinese food he wanted from the Chinese cooks in the kitchen."

Eighteen days later, after a brief stop in Yokohama, Japan, and an endless stretch crossing the vast North Pacific, the *Empress of Asia* docked in Vancouver on June 21, 1920, just over a century ago. He can't be sure, but Larry pictures Tim Hing being met by his father, who brought him to the farm on the Musqueam reserve where his new life would begin. But that may not be true; on one of his trips, possibly this first one, Tim Hing was put into quarantine on arrival, an ordeal that lasted one or two weeks and must have been terrifying.

We know all these details because Dr. Henry Yu, a historian at the University of British Columbia, has studied early Chinese immigration and found Hong Tim Hing's name in the ship's manifest. Except he wasn't registered as Hong Tim Hing; like many Chinese immigrants, the young man entered Canada under a false or "paper" name: Jang Gun Fun. Larry has no idea why that name or where that name came from; Chinese immigrants often bought certificates with the names of the real children of Canadian citizens or residents. Either way, his father was a "paper son," a relative who entered Canada illegally under some-one else's name. Even after an amnesty in 1960, the "Chinese Adjustment Statement Program," this fact would discourage many Chinese immigrants from ever going back to China, for fear that they would never be able to return to Canada.

Dr. Yu and a research team helped put together a database with the names of all ninety-seven thousand people—all Chinese, mostly men—who paid the Head Tax over the thirty-eight years it was enforced, based on records kept by Canadian immigra-tion officials. The handwritten "General Register of Chinese Immigration" shows that Jang Gun Fun paid five hundred dollars in cash on arrival. Larry doesn't know where he got that mon-ey—a huge sum, equivalent to eight thousand dollars today—but imagines that his grandfather and other relatives had saved it up, and Hong Tim Hing / Jang Gun Fun then had to work for them to pay off his debt. Many Chinese immigrants spent years or even decades working off their loans, a form of indentured labour.

Tim Hing was lucky he owed his family, not some unscrupulous farmer or restaurant owner. The coal baron Robert Dunsmuir, a Scot who immigrated to British Columbia in 1851, paid the Head Tax and passage fees for Chinese miners, then paid them far less than white miners and used them as scabs to break strikes; he died the richest man in BC, a cabinet minister and proud resident of a fake-Scottish folly, Victoria's Craigdarroch Castle.

////////////////

That's how Hong Tim Hing found himself ten thousand kilometres from the village of his birth, growing vegetables on a small plot of lush soil on the banks of the Fraser River in Musqueam Reserve No. 2. Larry remembers the farm and the wooden farmhouse, which was bulldozed to make way for houses in the 1960s. "One side was a bunkhouse, and next to it was an outdoor area where the men washed the vegetables, crated them and loaded them onto trucks. In my youth our dad was the teamster—he drove the truck and looked after the gasoline equipment." Gas-driven water pumps were a relatively recent innovation; in the first decades the men worked with wooden implements brought over from China, hand- or foot-driven but still useful.

Larry's great-uncle told him about how the first Chinese men to live on the reserve became involved in the Musqueam winter dances. They heard the drums beating in the night, and one evening one of the men was overcome with curiosity and knocked on the door of one of the Big Houses and asked if Larry's grandfather Seymour, who they leased the land from, was around. Seymour invited him and his brothers in, and the men were soon regular participants.

"When they knocked, things would sort of quieten down in the Big House, and in would walk my father and my great-uncles, carrying fruit and vegetables to donate to the host of whatever cultural activity was taking place," Larry says. He adds that the ceremonies were "very, very similar to their culture, back in the Cantonese-speaking area of China where they came from. They were there to contribute. My great-uncle always used to tell us they do ceremonies with masks, 'faith healing,' in China too. So they were very supportive of all of those things."

A family photo from the time shows Larry's father sitting with some other Chinese men in a fancy room in Chinatown. He is wearing a three-piece suit with a fashionable thin tie. Tall and square-jawed, with straight dark hair and full, unsmiling lips, he is a serious and handsome young man, a man on a mission.

Another family photo shows Agnes Grant standing outside between her sister Edna and a cousin, before the sisters left home. All three have styled their thick black hair in fashionable bobs and have long woollen skirts and proud expressions. Agnes wears a thick silver bracelet carved with Musqueam designs and holds a big rectangular handbag. She is an elegant young woman who looks at ease in the world.

"My father worked right by the main road on the reserve, and he used to see her walking back and forth, usually by herself or with other ladies, but never with a male person," says Larry. "So he found out she must be single."

Intrigued and attracted, Tim Hing found out which house this mysterious young lady came from and went down there, always accompanied by an older person, a matchmaker or spokesperson, following Chinese custom. "He started visiting with my grandparents, my mother's parents. And all the time, it's my mother that he wants to take for a wife. The Musqueam custom was that you didn't choose your own mate, they were chosen for you, because of resource sharing—a lot of families of status would marry into another family at their level. And that also was part of Chinese culture—but he also knew that he had to go and ask himself, so he was down there . . . I don't know how many years he was down there negotiating with my grandparents."

Agnes eventually learned the news from her mother, and at first she was nonplussed. She was in her late twenties by then (the same age as her suitor) and quite happy being single; she'd seen most of her friends married off and had no desire to do the same. As the oldest daughter, she helped her mother look after her two younger sisters. She had seen what a burden this was and didn't want the responsibility of her own family as well. She did all the family laundry and made some money cooking and cleaning, all of which went to her parents, who clothed and fed her. She also felt too old to have children.

At that time, a century ago, the whole community still spoke hən̓q̓əmin̓əm̓, and Agnes was known for her rich vocabulary and knowledge of traditional stories and rituals. This came with various responsibilities, including being the family historian who knew the genealogy and traditional names of all the main Musqueam families—an important duty in Indigenous society, as names come with rights such as fishing, hunting or territorial privileges. People came to visit her all the time to discuss matters of protocol. They also came to her if they needed to know a word that had been forgotten, like the name of an animal, plant or emotion. People would say, "Go speak to Agnes, she knows," Larry says.

Larry's sister, Helen Callbreath, who carries Agnes's traditional name θəwəχəlwət today, remembers that when she and her brothers were young, her mother would always remind them who they were and where they came from. "Now you listen," she would say, "Musqueam is your anchor. You will be the ones to remember the teachings and pass them on to the younger ones."

Looking back, Larry understands his mother's reticence about the marriage proposal. "You get to an age where, yeah, circumstances are not really there for you to have children or responsibility. She worked her heart and her soul out for her children, and we got to realize how much she had sacrificed because she had a double load—well, maybe a triple load. She had a dreamer for a husband, a gambler; and she had the load of her siblings and her parents. Quite a load."

But at the time she had no choice in the matter. Her parents told her, "This fellow wants to marry you," and next thing she knew she had a husband. The decision was made. "Marriages were arranged still," Larry says. "She's one of the last ones that we know of that was arranged. They said, 'That's your husband.'"

The actual wedding ceremony—which didn't take place until 1940, after they had been together for seven years and had three children—was a strange affair. It was held at the Chinese Presbyterian Church at Keefer Street and Gore Avenue in Chinatown, founded in 1895 (it moved to Oakridge in the 1980s). Agnes Grant didn't even know she was getting married that day. "Dad just said, 'Get dressed up. We're going to town.' When he talks to you in Chinese, you just say, 'Yes.'" Larry chuckles and shakes his head. "And she did.

"It was all in Chinese. She just said 'Yep' and that was it. And then they were married, but she didn't know that because she couldn't read or write in Chinese or English. She didn't understand."

All this because Agnes had only gone to residential school for a year before her father, seeing what it was really like, took her and both of her sisters out. "I don't know how he achieved that," Larry says. "Apparently he told them, 'Go ahead, put me in jail, the kids aren't going back.'" So Larry's mother never did learn to read English; like her family and many others in Musqueam, she relied on interpreters to read or write important documents for her.

It wasn't a love match, but Larry thinks she grew to love him. She hadn't wanted a spouse, but then she had one—an absentee spouse who spent most of his time in Chinatown, where he owned part of a warehouse and often slept in friends' or relatives' apartments. And because she had been raised with a sense of responsibility, in a culture where it was the parents' job to pick a mate for their children, she accepted their decision. And that man, her spouse, wanted to be the father of her children, so she felt a responsibility towards him, however big a dreamer he was.

Asked how his parents communicated, Larry replies, "Probably by the old international rules of love, I don't know!" His mother didn't have an accent in English, but his father spoke like he was four or five years old, he says. "He was heavily influenced with the Chinese language, in that he couldn't form specific words or letters, like 'Vancouver' or 'Larry' or 'Gordie'—they were missing Rs and Ls and letters transposed back and forth. Mother didn't speak that way; she could speak just like we are right now. But my grandparents, they didn't speak very much English," just hәṅ̓q̓әmiṅ̓әm̓ or Cantonese.

"She did have feelings for him," Larry says. "We saw that when he passed away. We didn't realize it was that deep. We, I, thought it was a partnership of convenience, a sharing of resources." Larry and his siblings—his elder brother Gordon and his younger sister and brother Helen and Howard—used to joke, "Yep, my mum's married to the Chinese gardener, and we get vegetables all year long." But it was deeper than that.

"She grieved for him in a way that we weren't expecting, y'know, it was something to see. It did grow into love, out of respect for who she was and where she came from. And out of respect for his culture that she did grow into, and to love him that way."

Whenever Larry or his siblings said something derogatory about their often-absent dad, their mother would say, "No, that's your father. You can't help who he is. You can't do that. It's not your choice, that's what you are: half Chinese, half Indian."

"Well, half Chinese, part Indian, and part Scotch," says Larry with a laugh.

"Scotch?" I ask. "Like me?" My maternal grandparents were Frasers, like the river and Simon the explorer, which amuses Larry.

"Yeah, that's the 'Grant'," he replies. The family has since established that John or Jack Grant, known as "Captain Jack," was a Scottish soldier who led a group of Royal Engineers sent to Vancouver Island in 1858, just before the gold rush; and that about two years later, he became the father of Larry's grandfather Seymour.

Larry's great-grandmother, ce:yqa:t, met Captain Jack at lyaqsən on Galiano Island, one of the Gulf Islands between Vancouver and Vancouver Island, by what is now called Porlier Pass; she and her sister had fled there to hide from Indigenous raiders from the north who were wreaking havoc in the Salish Sea. She had a boy called Seymour, and when Captain Grant learned he was being sent back to Britain, he proposed taking his son home with him.

"He offers to take his son back to Britain and raise him up as a Scottish boy!" Larry says, shaking his head. "His mother refuses and he waves goodbye and that's the last we know of him. Except for the name. My grandfather carries the name 'Seymour Grant.' And that's what we are.

"Yeah, I'm one-eighth Scottish, half Chinese, straight eights həṅq̓əmiṅəṁ.

"I wish I knew where in Scotland he was from. Not to go there. Just to know."

Back in Agassiz, Larry looks out towards the spectacular Coast Mountains and downs the dregs of his coffee. We've been debating going back to find more evidence of Hamersley's Hopyard, but it's too cold, and he admits he's not that bothered anyway.

Instead we bundle back into the car and begin the long drive home, on the Highway 7 scenic route, following the winding river westward to the sea.

Chapter Two

Growing Up Musqueam /
On Reserves No. 1 and 2

Larry's first memories go back to his time on the reserve, when he was about three years old. The first that truly sticks in his mind is playing in the middle of summer, in front of his grandpa's Big House, while his mother was doing the wash outside. He started walking around saying, "Look Mum! Look Mum! Got a broken leg." He had a stick with a crook on it and was using it as a crutch.

His mum said, "Don't be foolish. You're going to get a broken leg if you keep fooling like that."

Later that afternoon, Larry saw a truck coming down the dirt road. It belonged to a Chinese man with a farm a block away, who had given the boy a candy every day he came home that summer. So Larry ran across the road towards it. "My mother was yelling at me to wait," he says, "but being the little boy that wanted that candy, I ran in behind the vehicle and got run over, and had my left leg broken. Ahh!"

He spent a month or two recuperating in the hospital. The farmer that owned the truck paid his mother three hundred dollars, but unfortunately his father got hold of the cash and used it as a gambling stake and blew it all in one night.

That was the first, conscious beginning of Larry's memories. He's never forgotten his mother's connection between playing at something and making it real—a scary concept for a small child. He's also grown to accept another thing she used to say: little children have huge memory banks, they absorb so much knowledge and history and when they grow up to be adults, all these latent memories emerge. "You make sure you speak correctly to these little people," she used to say, "because they have minds that can remember."

Larry also has memories of his grandfather Seymour's house from that time, when he was still only about three years of age. It was on the river side of the Big House, what some people call the "longhouse" now. Attached to it was a horse barn just large enough for one horse. His grandfather's house was only about twelve feet wide and twenty-five or thirty feet long. He remembers his uncles, his mother's brothers, gathered in there: Austin, who was called Uncle Oster; Uncle Bill, whose real name was Felix; and Uncle Jimmy.

Behind that was another house that belonged to his uncle Sam, Larry's qəyplenəxʷ (his mother's older brother). There was also a woodshed, which held about four cords of wood; a chicken coop, home to about twenty chickens; and Grandpa Andrew's Big House right next door, which had a one-room kitchen and living area attached to it. (Grandpa Andrew wasn't Larry's grandfather in the English sense; he was Larry's grandmother's younger half-brother.)

Larry's grandfather, Seymour Grant, was a much-respected leader in the community. Over the course of his long life he had been a logger, a fisherman, an itinerant hop picker and a cultural authority who gave one of the last great potlatches before they were banned. By the time Larry knew him—when he was in his late seventies and early eighties—he was best known as a boat builder.

Grandpa had what everyone called a "floathouse," a house on logs about ten feet wide by sixteen feet long. Larry never saw it happen, but every summer Grandpa got it towed upriver to a beach near where the Pattullo Bridge and Brownsville Bar are today; at the time this was Musqueam Indian Reserve No. 1. Larry's other early memories, shimmery happy memories, are of his childhood summers spent there, with his mother θəwəχəlwət (Agnes), his auntie ʔeýxʷaθəyə (Edna), his older brother Gordon, his older cousin Sally (whose real name was Margaret) and her younger sister Anita. The floathouse was tied to the shore and went up and down with the tide. "The six or seven of us would all be in that little house," Larry recalls. "We basically lived off the fish that my grandfather caught in the river," mostly salmon and massive white sturgeon.

The kids spent all their time in the back eddy or qeyqəyt, swimming and playing while the adults got ready for salmon season to begin. He says "swimming" but then corrects it to "wading"—no one in the family could swim, Larry included, except one uncle who used to set out regularly across the Fraser and back. "We just splashed around," Larry says, "until one time when I got the shit scared out of me."

The kids were playing one day in the water at a little island near the Alex Fraser Bridge, about a kilometre downriver from Reserve No. 1. "There was a cement plant there, and a big back eddy," Larry recalls. "I was fourteen years old, jumping off a float into water about this deep," he says, putting his hands at waist height. "Thought I could swim. I was diving in, coming out, diving in. Then someone caught me unawares, I got shoved in and panicked. Never went in the water again for about ten years."

The beach where his grandpa moored the floathouse is still there, now part of a dingy little park, Brownsville Bar Park. A sign by the entrance reads, "Welcome to the City of Surrey: The Future Lives Here." Larry is on the beach now, for the first time in decades, feeling nostalgic and more than a little sad. It's changed so much that it's taken him a while to find the right spot. Above us looms the great bulk of the Pattullo Bridge, one of the city's biggest commuter arteries, casting its shadow over the grey sand and the filthy brown river swollen with early spring runoff.

"All this development, the huge industry here, there was none when we were kids," he says. "Sawmills, cement works. The reserve went up the hill here." He shivers in the February cold, made worse by the humidity. No wonder they only came here in summer.

"Now it's all lumber yards, train tracks," I add.

"Yup, all industrial. 'The Future,' oh yeah, it's growin' fast. The back eddy where we played was back in there." Now a concrete SkyTrain bridge towers overhead, one of four bridges nearby. The oldest one, the rail bridge, used to be covered in planks so that cars could drive over between trains. Larry remembers the noises at night, lying in bed in the floathouse listening to the clack-clack of the planks and the toot-toot of the trains. "Chug a chug," he says with a wan smile.

"What man has done to nature," he adds, shaking his head at the grim industrial vista all around us. "How beautiful this river used to be, once upon a time. It's been a working river ever since colonization. But the beaches are still here." Not that you'll be seeing these ones in WestJet ads any time soon.

The Department of Indian Affairs dissolved Musqueam Indian Reserve No. 1 in 1949, on the grounds that no band members had permanent settlements there. Summer holidays and floathouses didn't pass muster.

"What gave them the right to do that?"

"White privilege," answers Larry. Unlike me, he's not shocked. He's used to it.

///////////////

When Larry was about eight years old, Grandpa moved the float-house, repositioning it on Reserve No. 2 along the front side of the community's Big House. By then he also had the family's Big House, plus a work shed, a wooden shack the size of a single garage five or ten yards west of the horse barn where he built boats. As a boy, Larry was already fascinated by tools and making things and was always sneaking into the boathouse to watch the old man at work. "And Grandpa was always chasing me out of the way," he recalls with a laugh. "He built double-ended boats about thirty feet long, what we called 'gas boats' at that time. Engine-powered."

His grandfather's Big House stood on the upland part of the reserve near what is now the clubhouse of Shaughnessy Golf Club. It had two rooms downstairs—the living room and the kitchen—and the upstairs was one large sleeping area. "It was just like a dorm up there—my grandfather, my family always sleeping together, in separate beds but all in the same room," he says. "I slept with my brother 'til I was twenty-one, twenty-two years, just a regular single bed. My sister had her own bed and there was a double bed for mum and dad. That was it. Except every bed had a feather mattress—duck feathers, not chicken feathers."

These mattresses were so fluffy, the kids played hide-and-seek by climbing up on a trunk, diving into them and disappearing. "You could lie down and cover up, and it would appear as if no one was in the bed!" Larry says with a big laugh. "Just playing a trick. You'd go to bed early sometimes just to fool around."

"When you looked from the front of that house on a clear day, you could see Vancouver Island." Larry's not sure if that was intentional, but he's since learned that his grandfather's roots are lyackson, a closely related Coast Salish Nation from Valdes Island, south of present-day Nanaimo on Vancouver Island. "I don't know if that's the reason he built where he did. It seemed odd to me that the house was built maybe fifty feet from the edge of the cliff—why would you do that? But I was a kid then, so . . ." The house was demolished when the Shaughnessy golf course was built in the late 1950s, on reserve land leased by the Indian agent at a fraction of its value.

Larry remembers his grandmother preparing the *swiwa*, the oily fish known in Chinook jargon as *eulachon* and in English as *oolichan* or *candlefish*, in her family's Big House. Like small herring, the oolichan used to gather in huge runs. The family would have tubs and tubs of the greasy little fish, and Granny would skewer them on cedar sticks and hang them up around a smouldering fire to dry them for the winter. She also prepared the salmon harvest in there with Larry's mother and her sisters in the fall. "My aunties would be doing all of the work on the fish. And my grandfather and my uncles would be out there getting the food. . . . They had the winter dances in there, but she also did all the food preparation and preservation in that same house."

Larry can still hear and smell his mother cooking duck, a staple in the Musqueam diet back then. "When she was butchering, you could actually smell the blood and the body odour of the ducks," he says. "She would singe them in the kitchen stove fire and you smell the pin feathers burning, and you begin to salivate, because you can just taste the finished product right away." It was the same with fish—salmon, herring, sturgeon—the tasty smell as they were being baked or fried. But the nicest smell, the one that reminds him most of his mother, is oolichan frying. "It has a very particular, very soft smell—I guess today, you would compare it to French fries."

Oolichan are rolled in flour and salt and then fried whole. "They're not gutted or anything, they're not cleaned, they're not headed, their tails aren't taken off," says Larry. "They're so rich in oil that it basically renders the fish, and the oil in the pan just gets deeper and deeper and deeper. They're actually fried in their own fat." When the little fish are done to perfection, the tail and skin are really crispy. Some people, including Larry's big brother Gordon, eat them whole, head, tail, guts and all, but back then Larry never could; the thought of the guts was too much. Nowadays he swallows them whole in the traditional way.

All up and down the coast, Indigenous people render oolichan to get the oil, which they put on everything they eat. "Pork chops, apple pie, berries, other fish, dried food, they dip it in oolichan oil, which has the same qualities as cod liver oil," says Larry. "Very healthy. They even use it as cough medicine."

"When we were lucky enough to be with our father," Larry adds, "it was often in the bunkhouse, which we called 'the cook-shack.' And we would eat Chinese food. Our *gung*, or great-uncle, was one of the best cooks we ever had. He cooked for ten guys, morning, noon and night." Larry remembers playing in the fields with his brothers and cousins in the evenings and hearing great-uncle ring the bell to tell everybody dinner was ready. They would all rush back to the cook-shack and wash up and then join the men for a delicious meal. He loved sitting there with his father and uncles and being accepted as one of them.

A photo shows the Chinese men, and one woman, having dinner in that farmhouse kitchen. They are sitting at a wooden table covered in linoleum, eating with chopsticks from white porcelain bowls, laughing and talking. On the walls are five or six calendars, two from the Bank of Montreal: one features a curvy Hollywood pin-up in a skin-tight dress, another a stick-thin, designer-dressed model in front of the Eiffel Tower. A telephone hangs on the far wall, next to a blackboard with columns of notes in Chinese script.

Larry's father worked really hard, which meant that he rarely saw his children, except sometimes on Sunday afternoons. Larry can't say for certain, but he suspects he had to work so much to pay off his Head Tax debt to his father and uncles. "These guys got up in the morning at, y'know, four o'clock in the summertime," Larry says. "Get up, eat, go to work, probably long after sundown before they ate supper. Never stop to pray, not even on Sundays. They'd go to town on Sundays, that was the only time. Used to be a Chinese travelling barber came around to give a haircut to the farmers."

Larry has always liked Chinese food best of all, because it reminds him of his dad and of his great-uncle's wonderful cooking. And there's a third reason: "There's so much variety of the animals that you eat—the insides, and the meat from the outside. I really appreciate that." A lot of his relatives who went to residential school got used to the Eurocentric diet there and were no longer able to eat game or offal, even though the Musqueam had always hunted a wide variety of wild animals and eaten every part of them. "Some of them make all kinds of faces when you tell them what you're eating," Larry says with glee. "They say, 'Oh, how can you eat that?' It's protein, it's animal protein. It has a different, distinct flavour that we grew up with. It's really nothing to shy away from. And you don't throw away a good portion of the animal, you use the whole thing."

Like at his grandparents' place, in the cook-shack kitchen, whatever was on the table, you had to taste it—not eat it, necessarily, but at least taste it. "And if you reached over with your chopsticks to grab something out of a dish, you couldn't move things away to get at the thing that you *really* desired," Larry says with a childish laugh. "You had to take what was on top and eat it. You couldn't *move* things with your chopsticks to get at them, a special piece of meat or a special vegetable that you liked; you had to wait until you got down to it, and then if you weren't quick enough, you didn't get it!"

Larry's mother Agnes also learned some recipes and techniques from Larry's *gung*, her uncle-in-law. "They were fairly close, and he explained to her how to cook. She gradually got to be a pretty good Chinese cook." They couldn't get many sauces and spices on the farm, so it was a very straightforward, Cantonese style of cooking. "Caucasian Chinese," Larry calls it. "Very plain-tasting. And when Dad was coming to dinner, lots of vegetables."

⁓⁓⁓⁓⁓⁓

Larry says that a lot of the young people today can't relate to the fact that the Big Houses were not only ceremonial, but they were also used as group residences, like co-op housing. "Those were the original homes of our people, they were not just something to do with ceremony; it was actually a complete house where you lived, slept, ate and preserved all your winter food, and did all your oral history and your winter dancing. A lot of people today speak about our Big House as our 'church,' but it is more than that."

He has no memory of his people praying together in the Big House, at least not the way many of them pray today, where they will get up and say a Christian grace for the food all together in the Western way. His mother taught him that each person is responsible for their own spirituality and their own self-worth— you should be thanking the "creator" every day that you wake up so that every day you give thanks, not just on Sundays. And you don't need to do that together, you can do it out in the woods or out at sea. Anywhere that you get up you give thanks for being awake and alive that day, and ask for things that will make the lives of you and your family better.

The only time Larry remembers any sort of prayer gathering was when the Indian agent was coming down. Word spread on the "moccasin telegraph," as they called it: "The Indian agent is in the area, he's down the road, everybody stop your singing because now we have to pray because we can't be together like this if it's not a prayer meeting." Ever since the Potlatch Ban started being enforced, any non-Christian gatherings were strictly forbidden.

For Larry, the Big House is "not our 'church,' it's actually our place of life. And the spirituality of a person is their own concern, their own responsibility." If a person didn't live within the parameters of the society they were living in, they would be sent to another community, another little village, and told, "Those people act like that all the time, you go up there and see if you can handle being treated the way you're treating other people. And don't come back 'til you can act the way we act in this village." For him, that's part of the responsibility of spirituality.

"You have to remember, in our language we do not have words like God, devil, angel, heaven, hell, Jesus Christ," he adds. "Even the word *creator*—of what? All these are adopted words."

"The belief of our people is that everything in our world has a spirit power that controls its life," Larry explains, "and that's how we're all connected to the natural world. The rocks, the fish, the mountains, the land, the trees we cut down to make canoes, the sea life we eat—everything has a spirit power, or soul, to use the Western word. Rocks aren't dead; mountains erupt, lava flows, there's landslides, you see all of that on the way to Whistler! There's a reason why everything moves—it's all alive, and we're all connected to it, part of it."

In the Musqueam worldview, everything in your life happens for a reason, and even the negative things may be good for you, because they change your focus into something more positive. "We believe in karma," says Larry. "If you're a shit all your life, that's what you are going to get back! If you're a good person, you'll get that back."

Larry never saw his grandfather say grace at a meal. The reason given to him at the time was that, whenever a hunter goes to get deer or fish or any other animal, he prepares himself with a four-day ritual of bathing and cleansing his body and his mind. That includes not being with his wife or girlfriend for four days. He would ask the spirit of the hunted animal to be kind to him and to give themselves up to him so that he could live and feed his people. And then, when he was ready, he would go out hunting, and when he killed a deer or an elk or a bird, he would thank it for being kind to him and allowing him to take its life, and he would pay respects to it at the moment of its death. "That's why in Indigenous culture, there is no need to say grace at mealtime, because that thanks has already been given, to the spirit of the animal by the person who took its life, not by the one who has received the food down the line somewhere.

"That's the spirituality that my mother and my grandparents spoke of," Larry says. "It's every day of your life, it's not, you go out and do whatever you want during the week, and on Sunday you go to church to be absolved of all the wrong things you have done. The core of my belief is that churches are a place of gathering and more of a control thing than of concern for your individual spirituality. And if you had the right teachings from your ancestors and your parents and your peers, there's no real problem with your spirituality." He remembers his mother praying every day, giving thanks that she was alive and that her children and family were all well.

His mother and her family had healthy attitudes towards the body and sexuality, Larry says. "It's a normal biological function—all you need to do is control it. You can talk about it all you want. In the mixed company of my mother's peers and my grandparents' peers it was like walking into an adult bar!" he says with a laugh. "Everybody's talking about sex and bodily functions and sexual abilities. It was really different to be in a house full of people that were not truly converted into European society.

"It was the fun part of life," he continues. "'Ha, ha, ha! He can't control himself, he's always doin' this.' 'Yeah, but he can't help it, that's just how he is, or how she is.' It was just everyday practical joking, but they also accepted the humanness of each other."

Larry's mother also taught her children to only do something if their hearts were really in it. His younger brother Howard, for instance, was always a good speaker who bloomed in front of people. "So that was it, OK," says Larry. "You got the words, you got the thoughts, and you have the desire to be standing in front of people, so that's what you'll do." His older brother Gordon was very different. "He had a lot of responsibilities, which took him away from being a child. So now, in his later life, he doesn't get out and talk to people." Instead, he helps behind the scenes: "He is a backroom type of person who has difficulties expressing who he is."

As for Larry, he hung around his grandfather all the time and always knew he would become a tradesperson. And not one specific type of a tradesperson: "My grandfather built boats, he could build houses, and he did a lot of other cultural things, and I was always close to him. It was easy for me to be a Shell Busey type of person, a Mr. Fix-It who gives you the right gutters, the right furnace. An all-round tradesperson. He may not be completely trained in everything, but he is trained enough to move from one trade into another and hold it all together. That's always been my life.

"A lot of this happened prior to any training that I got in high school," he says. "It was just watching my grandfather and noticing the other old people in the village at that time, just going about surviving. All those survivor skills came out of my head as I grew older. People would ask me, 'Well, how come you know about this, you analyze it just by looking at it?' And you say, 'Well, yeah, it goes together like this, so, if that other part is broken, it comes apart that way. I can repair it and put it back together, that's it!'" That's what he's done since he was a child, with gutters and furnaces and diesel engines, but also with culture and language: fixing things, helping people out.

"That's something our old people always did," Larry says. There were a few specific things they didn't share, like a lot of the traditional medical practices. But every other bit of knowledge they acquired was always passed on, to make life less arduous. He carried this on into his own life, working to hand down the teachings of his grandparents and his mother. "If you really want to help people, you have to give them every bit of knowledge you have," he says. "That helps them to be a good person, and makes you a good person, because you're willing to share. My grandfather's life was like that, he always shared his resources, his assets and his knowledge with his community and his family."

Larry was born too late to see it, but his family often talked about his grandfather's great sx̌ǝnǝq or potlatch, one of the last held in Musqueam before the ban started being enforced. "He potlatched for a whole week, fed the people from the neighbouring communities. And they just stayed there and sang and danced and potlatched. That's something that I've never ever seen in my life, but that's a piece of history that was passed on to me from my mother."

At the sx̌ǝnǝq, Larry's grandfather, Seymour Grant or xʷǝpqʷǝlecǝ, gave a traditional name to his daughter, Larry's mother: θǝwǝx̌ǝlwǝt (Agnes). He also gave her sisters ancestral names: skʷǝliθǝyeʔ (Margaret) and ʔeýx̌ʷaθǝyǝ (Edna). Then there were gifts for all the visitors, including food and blankets, which were stacked on a platform between two towering house posts and handed out to the crowd assembled below. "He had blankets in there, laid out flat on the floor, and each pile of blankets in front

of each girl was as high as the girls were tall. The part that's missing in that memory is whether they were Hudson's Bay blankets
or if they were swəq̓ʷəɫ, the goat's wool blankets." Thinking about
the legislated poverty and dependency that has replaced grand
events like this fills Larry with immense sadness.

All this took place sometime between 1916 and 1920, when
Larry's mother was about twelve years old. The grandfather
Larry remembers was a very thin man with a slim face and a little
hook nose who was very active and always on the move. In 1942,
he was still racing his grandchildren. Larry remembers being
sent to tell him dinner was ready, when he was about six and
Gordie was eight and their grandfather must have been eighty-
two or more. "Grandpa would say, 'I'll race you guys home.' It
was about five hundred metres, and he'd give us a fifty-metre
head start and we'd all be running for what we'd be worth—and
he would pass us and beat us to the house. Just laughing, 'Ah, I
can still beat you guys!'"

Larry's grandmother, Mary Charlie, made cedar-bark and
spruce-root baskets of all sizes by hand. It was slow, patient
work, often done in a group of women. "They would walk up the
Dunbar area, around 41st Avenue, and exchange baskets for food,
money or clothing," in the 1930s and '40s, says Larry. In the fall
they would also collect berries—wild blackberries, salal berries,
huckleberries, salmon berries in the spring—and go around the
neighbourhood door to door, exchanging or selling them. "The
fruit, along with the baskets."

When Larry was young, his older brother Gordon remembers
walking with their grandmother from Reserve No. 1 over the
Pattullo Bridge up onto Royal Avenue in New Westminster to
go house to house, knocking on doors and asking people if they

would like to trade some food or an article of used clothing for a basket.

Larry's grandmother was a very loving person, but "she was always serious about life," he says. "Life is this way, this is what you have to do and this is how you behave when people are around. And if you have a problem with the kids outside, talk it out, don't just start fighting." So it was serious—unlike Grandpa, Grandma didn't play. She ruled with him. "Grandpa was the boss, and she was the boss at the same level," Larry recalls. "They were partners, equal partners in life. She had equal say in everything that happened in the house and in the family."

That said, when visitors arrived, Grandma would take the subservient role in front of them. Larry doesn't know if that was a post-contact thing or Musqueam tradition. His grandfather was born sometime around 1860—there is no accurate written record—around the same time as the Fraser Gold Rush (1858) and the arrival of the first European settlers in what would become Vancouver (McCleery's Farm in Marpole, 1862), and about seven years before Canada was created through Confederation (1867; British Columbia wouldn't join until 1871). The Musqueam world has changed so much since then, it's hard to know where to begin.

Even in the early 1940s, when Larry was a boy, the community was unrecognizable from what it is today. There weren't many people for one thing—a couple of hundred, compared to more than 1,700 band members today. As well as his grandfather's cluster of houses and Grandpa Andrew's house next door, there was Lizzy Robert's parents—and then there wasn't another house for ages. A little eastward were Henry Louis and his family and the French Louie; the next house belonged to a

Chinese farmer, on the spot where a tall, wide stump used as a house pole once stood.

The stump in question, which ended up in the golf course and has since been removed, marked the spot where an earlier Big House once stood. The stump's high, flattened top was used to hold all the gifts. "That's where the swəq̓ʷəł, the wool blankets, were heaped in piles, on top of that board," Larry says. "They would throw them away to the crowd at a potlatch. It's a scramble, your wealth is so great you can just throw it away. Ah, that's how they did it then. They would throw all of that stuff away." He makes a throwing motion, like passing a rugby ball, and laughs with glee thinking about it.

These great events took place in the time of the salmon, around August, when food was plentiful. People would come together from all the different communities on Vancouver Island and far upriver. Usually the potlatch would be thrown by one family or even just one person. If it was the family, they would all be there together; if there was only one person taking the credit, their whole family may have contributed but he or she alone would be recognized as the host. Most potlatches took place in the summer, unlike spirit dancing, sometimes called winter dancing.

After about 1920, when the authorities started enforcing the federal government's Potlatch Ban of 1885, all of this went inside and underground.

///////////

As a young boy, Larry remembers asking his mother, "If Grandfather was so wealthy, how come we're poor?"

"Because of the customs of the day," she replied. "Being rich was being able to share, so we actually gave away everything, except for the things we needed to survive." Larry's grandfather gave away all the goods he ever owned. And not just at his potlatch; it was a normal way to live. When Larry was born, the community was cash-poor because very few people were able to acquire stable, year-round jobs. "All the work was seasonal, so you had to save a lot of money for winter, or can or dry a lot of goods," Larry says. "My idea of rich was someone who could afford to go and buy anything they wanted. And we couldn't, so we started to work and would eat up cash: a pair of shoes in September, a new jacket, a new toque. Then that was it. You end up looking around in the thrift shop rather than the new one next door. How come we're shopping in the thrift shop all the time if Papa's so rich?"

But for Larry's Musqueam family, richness was all about your cultural knowledge, your understanding of your family's extended genealogy. "It's knowing all of the cultural things that you need to know, the things that are part of your land that you are living on. That is part of your richness. It wasn't monetary, it was all of that cultural and kinship knowledge. It's important to know who you are, where you come from, how you belong to the cultural activities that you perform in. And know all of your extended family. That was considered being rich.

"Worldly goods are for someone who is greedy, doesn't know how to look after others rather than just looking after oneself. That's the difference from what I call the refugee immigrant settler mindset, where to be rich is to have enough money to be able to control other people's lives, make them work for you."

He looks off into the distance, where a gentle wind is still swaying the poplar trees by the river. He's thinking of true wealth, the kind no money can buy: a loving mother, telling him to be proud to be Musqueam; the excited stories of his grandfather's potlatch; the bell summoning him and his brothers to dinner in the cook-shack with his father and uncles; all those hən̓q̓əmin̓əm̓-speaking aunts and uncles whose doors and arms were always open.

An idyllic little boy's life on the reserve, about to be disrupted forever.

Chapter Three

Cold-Water Flats /
In Chinatown

"This front part here was a fruit wholesaler," says Larry. "It looks like they changed the side. There's a hallway that goes to the back of the building, we lived there. That's probably the longest we lived in any one spot in Chinatown. In this building, Arno Rooms."

He's standing in front of a four-storey brick building on East Georgia Street just by the corner of Gore Avenue, on the eastern edge of Vancouver's Chinatown, looking unsure of himself. Is this the same place? The sidewalk is crowded, though less than it used to be, bustling with shoppers with carts, young professionals on their phones and delivery people talking in Cantonese while they wheel dollies laden with fruit and vegetables out of beeping trucks. The fruit wholesaler is now Tasty Market and Café, a trendy coffee shop and bulk food grocery with garage doors and green painted woodwork. Above are three levels of brick apartments topped by a stone cornice. It's an elegant heritage building, like a Brooklyn brownstone in bad need of a facelift.

"We lived in these two rooms here," says Larry more excitedly. He's found something he truly recognizes. He's just around the corner on Gore, where he's spied the front of his old home, now decorated on the outside with a bright mural of vegetables. "This has been added onto it, this part. Used to be three little houses here. That's where Old Man Wilson lived, a Black guy."

"A lot of people lived in here then," Larry says. "Some of the kids who went to Strathcona [elementary school] lived with their parents, all in one room. It was really mixed: other Indigenous people and immigrants and Black people. There used to be a delicatessen here too."

Vancouver's Chinatown is the largest in Canada, and one of the oldest and most storied in North America. It began its life in the late 1850s during the gold rush boom and grew rapidly when the big wave of Chinese immigrants arrived to build the railroad, opening laundries, bakeries and grocery stores and finding safety and community here. By 1900 it covered four square city blocks and was home to two thousand Chinese, mostly Cantonese- and Toisanese-speaking men from the Pearl River Delta in Guangdong.

In September 1907 the whole neighbourhood was almost razed during riots in Vancouver, part of an anti-Asian rampage that spread up and down the West Coast from Alaska to California. It was rebuilt and boomed between the wars, and by the 1950s covered eight blocks all the way west to the Millennium Gate at Taylor Street, an elegant new entrance adorned with carved lions, bright mosaics and tiled roofs. But it began to decline in the following decades as residents moved out of the crowded downtown to middle-class suburbs like Surrey and Richmond—or even rich neighbourhoods like Kerrisdale and Dunbar when China started booming, Hong Kong was returned to China and wealthy Chinese immigrants started outnumbering poor ones. In the 1990s, a wave of middle-class immigrants bypassed Chinatown altogether and headed straight to the suburbs. More recently Chinatown has been hit hard by economic downturns, the city's housing and opioid crises, and the covid pandemic. Sitting right next to the Downtown Eastside, Canada's poorest neighbourhood and the epicentre of Vancouver's ongoing drug and homelessness emergency, hasn't helped.

Larry and his elder brother Gordon moved to Chinatown all of a sudden in 1940, when they were just four and six years old respectively. Two traumatic events chased them off the reserve: being struck off the Musqueam band "Indian List" and the threat of residential school.

When Gordon, Larry and Helen were born, they were entered in the membership roll kept by the Department of Indian Affairs. But when news reached the Indian agent that Agnes Grant had married a non-status man, he took away her "Indian" status— under the Indian Act, status was patriarchal—and struck all three of her children off the roll, labelling them "the bastard children of Agnes Grant." With one stroke of a bureaucrat's pen, Larry, who had lived the first four years of his life in the bosom of a huge and loving Musqueam family, became Chinese—and no longer Indigenous.

"You can see the lines on the 'Indian list,'" says Larry, "where our names were crossed out. My mother didn't find out about this until we were ready to go to school." (Decades later, Howard would see this original list, at the Indian Affairs office downtown, while he was gathering evidence to get the family's rights reinstated.)

As for his father, he didn't seem to understand that he didn't have any rights at all at the time. "Being Chinese, he couldn't vote, wasn't a citizen! He wasn't Canadian, wasn't anything.

"It was a really odd mindset for a child to understand," Larry continues. "It was like you didn't belong anywhere. The Canadian government didn't recognize Chinese as citizens at that time, and didn't recognize us, other than as bastard, half-breed children of our mother. You're not fully recognized as a citizen, never mind Chinese or Indian.

"As children, we knew everything about Musqueam culture, language, spirituality—and yet we were not considered Indian. That is quite a turmoil in your mind, to try and work it out. Well, what am I then?"

Larry and Gordon went through this purgatory together because when Larry had heard that his elder brother was going off to kindergarten without him, he had been gutted. "I was four years of age, and I cried so hard, my parents also put me in kindergarten!" he says with a hint of pride, shaking his head.

The other catalyst for the move to Chinatown came from the Catholic priest on the reserve. When he heard that Agnes was going to send her kids to school, he took her aside and told her to get them off the reserve so they wouldn't have to go to the dreadful "school" in Mission city: St. Mary's Indian Residential School, eighty kilometres to the east in the Fraser Valley. This turned out to be very good advice, as Larry's many cousins who *did* go to Mission soon found out; not purgatory but hell. Though as non-Indigenous children, Larry and his siblings weren't eligible to attend residential school anyway.

///////////////

"As a boy, this was a little butcher shop." We're on East Pender Street now, in the block east of Main, just past an alley where two homeless men are going through a dumpster. The restaurant on the corner today is a hipper version of a typical basic diner: Fat Mao Noodle Bar, advertised in English on one window and in Chinese on the other, in flashy yellow and red script. The logo is a smiling cat in a bib slurping down a noodle. Hungry patrons tuck into heaped bowls of broth, sitting at a counter that looks out onto the crowded street.

"Sometimes we'd be eating, and then behind the partition, there was a gambling joint. Mah-jong, keno, poker, whatever. Gambling den. There were quite a few of them, but this one was where our dad hung out."

Gambling was accepted behaviour then, Larry explains. Larry's mother didn't mind, though sometimes she'd send the kids to get their dad. There were so many Chinese men there without families, with no wives or girlfriends or children, that men outnumbered women by more than ten to one. "They were basically remote workers and they all hung out. They needed somewhere to be together," Larry says. "This was one of the places."

"Dad liked to gamble," says Larry's sister, Helen. "We knew we could find him one place. Because he was married to an Aboriginal, some people in Chinatown called him 'Chief.'"

Most of the time, Larry's dad and the other Chinese men were just passing the time gambling, but sometimes the bets escalated and they played for hundreds, even thousands of dollars. That's how their father lost his share in the family's warehouse—by losing a bet to H.Y. Louie, a businessman on the rise who ran a general store and would go on to buy the London Drugs chain.

This happened when Larry was still little, in his first or second year in Chinatown. Before then he and Gordie had hung out with their dad at the warehouse, on East Georgia Street between Main and Gore Avenue, where the family stored produce from Lin On

Yuen. He remembers playing there, sliding down a chute they had set up to move inventory from the upper floor to the lower floor: "Running up the stairs and sliding down that chute, and then one day being told, 'Get out of here.'

"'Why, we always come in here?'

"'It's not your dad's place anymore.' He no longer had a share."

/////////////

Larry and Gordie moved to Chinatown in 1940, as World War II was just heating up. For the next dozen years, they went back and forth between Chinatown and the reserve, usually living downtown during the week and in Musqueam on the weekends. All this time their mother continued to live on the reserve because of a loophole in the Indian Act; in the 1930s and '40s, Indigenous women who had lost their status could refuse the usual cash payment and stay on the band list, though they lost all their other rights as Indigenous people. Agnes did this, becoming a "red ticket woman," after the colour of her special treaty card.

For the first two years, their father paid for Gordie and Larry to board at a Cantonese family's house just east of Chinatown on East Keefer Street. The building is long gone, so Larry's not sure where it was exactly.

"We were not treated as well as their own children, even though they were supposed to be taking care of us," he says. "That is something that always stuck with me. We didn't get as much food—sometimes the 'real' children would slip us scraps under the table." He and Gordie shared a bedroom in the basement, and their mother would join them sometimes. "And Dad would move in and out or around or whatever, he was there now and again." Some nights they were three or even four in one bed.

His second Chinatown home was a rooming house in the 500 block of East Georgia, in what is now a park across Gore Avenue from the Arno Rooms. "I don't know if you've seen the rooming houses down there," he says. "They consisted of one room about the size of this room"—his hands spread to encompass the small office we're in—"that had a hot plate or a gas burner, a wash basin, and sometimes not even that. The water tap would be down the far end of the hallway, and the bathrooms would be maybe two toilets. Sometimes known as a cold-water flat." Looking back, it was a rundown room in a decrepit building smelling of mould and greasy cooking, but as a kid it was just normal.

The rent in Chinatown was always taken care of by their father—"I don't know how, because he never had money"—and every now and then he ate with them and slept the night, but usually he was down at the farm. "Or at some other lady's place—we knew that even as young children," says Larry. "Our mother was a very factual person in the sense that she didn't gloss over life as something in a fairy tale. If people were promiscuous, that's how she spoke of them, and not in a judgmental way, it was just a laying down of the facts: 'Well, you have to be careful of these people over here: this guy likes to sleep around, or this lady likes to sleep around, or they're mean to children,' or whatever. Things like that. She never would say, 'Well you shouldn't be there.'"

This was confusing, because she spoke very frankly about people's failings, but when those same people knocked on her door, she would welcome them in as if they were long-lost relatives and treat them with endless love and kindness. "I used to ask her, 'You just told me last week that that person is not very nice and does this and that.' But today you opened the door and said, 'C'mon in, sit down.' You made something to eat, you made some tea and you talked all day!

"And she'd say, 'Yeah, whatever he or she does, that's one thing; however, that person is in our house to visit us, it's our relative, and that's how you have to be.'" At a young age Larry found this very hard to understand, but decades later it reminds him of professional relationships: "Working with another person you have respect for each other; you may not respect them for their personal life, but your working lives are different.... I came to realize that that's what life is—you can't deny the relationships that are there, the connections."

Family relationships were very important to his mother, because in Musqueam culture, that's where you sit in the hierarchy. Whatever rights you have stem from the people you are connected or related to. "And you must maintain that, otherwise it all breaks down," Larry explains.

When Larry was ten, his parents surprised them all by having another baby, Howard, Larry's young brother. Howard never lived in Chinatown with his siblings; after he was born, their mother rarely left the reserve.

///////////////

Other than not being able to play in the warehouse, Larry and his siblings always knew the people nearby had their back. Everyone knew who they were and kept an eye on the two boys, and later their sister Helen too.

"The Chinese looked after each other," Larry says. "All of our neighbours, when we lived in the corner place [the Arno Rooms], they knew we were there by ourselves many times. Mum would be on the reserve and Dad would be out working. They made sure that we were safe. It was a community."

It helped that Larry and his brothers and sister were well behaved and rarely got into trouble. "We surprised them," he says with a chuckle. "It was like a real living neighbourhood. Neighbours looked after neighbours. Even if you were fighting, if something wasn't right somebody would be yelling at you somewhere," telling you to smarten up or look after your brother.

Larry and his siblings weren't just latchkey kids—from about the age of eight they were responsible for making their own food. So they learned how to cook, and in Musqueam, how to make a fire and take care of themselves outdoors. In Chinatown, there was always rice in the cupboard, and a few other staples like dried shrimp, dried mushrooms and canned corned beef. And when their mother had some money, she'd give them enough to buy groceries, calculated down to the penny. "The oldest brother was responsible for keeping everyone in line," says Larry. "He was our surrogate father. And we would eat lunch in the cafeteria at Strathcona [school], if there was enough money. I used to cook the breakfast and the supper under direction from my older brother. Under duress," he adds with a laugh.

Larry learned to cook from his mother on the reserve. She said, "You boys are old enough to cook, because you know how to make fire; you've been watching me all your lives so you must prepare yourselves for life, because who knows what kind of a wife you're going to get. You may not get a wife, you may get a wife that does not cook, you may get a wife that does not clean up, you may get a wife that doesn't do laundry. And you have to learn all these things so that you can have a good life together, however that works out."

"There was a little fish store here," says Larry. He's reached the corner of Pender and Gore. "Used to go in here, or the butcher next door, and say, 'Hey, I want twenty-five cents worth of this meat,' and then they would cut it out and I would take it home. Sometimes I would come here and get a little perch or something. I learned how to shop."

He holds out his hands for effect and continues, "But also, when you look at them, you have to look at their eyes and say, 'I don't want that one. Its eye doesn't look right.' Then take it home and scale it and gut it and steam it."

In Chinatown there was often no one home except the three young children. "We were the ones that had to keep control of our lives, from that time until we finished high school. We got ourselves up, made our own breakfast, went to school, sometimes came home at lunch time to make up a sandwich or whatever, then back to school." For four years during elementary school they also attended Cantonese school, at Keefer and Gore, from four 'til six. "We were basically taking care of ourselves, completely responsible for our well-being."

A few doors west on Pender Street, Larry stops outside a lively Irish pub. "There were warehouses here, bringing in vegetables and fruits that they grew in Victoria. Didn't see too many non-Chinese around Chinatown back then—not like it is today." As if to prove his point, a well-dressed white guy with an impressive beard and stovepipe jeans steps outside, hops on his electric scooter and heads off down Pender.

The next stop is Dollar Meat Store (元昌燒臘肉食公司), its windows so steamed up that we can barely see the whole roast pig or the roast chickens hanging on display. We step in so Larry can buy something for dinner; all this talk of cooking has made him hungry. The tiled walls go way up to high ceilings, festooned with rows of sausages. The smell of roast duck is powerful.

He admires the duck legs and pig snouts but settles on some sausage. "Usually we get those packs of noodles, one of these sausages all cut up, some vegetables—that's a meal. There's a lot of shrimp and little fishes that they would dehydrate in a pack and add that to whatever else they're cooking." Larry has always loved to cook, even when he was very young.

/////////////

When they were a bit older, Gordie and Larry helped their dad deliver the produce from the farm. That meant waking up at four in the morning on the farm to help load the truck, then making stops at produce stores in the Dunbar and Kerrisdale neighbourhoods and on Macdonald Street, and finally home to Chinatown. When they were finished, they'd have breakfast in a greasy spoon—the highlight for the boys, sitting with the men as they smoked and joked—and then go home for a nap.

Larry remembers his father taking him along with Gordie and falling asleep all the way downtown. We could hear you snoring half a block away, Gordie always joked.

In the early days, one of the first stops was at the little corner store their grandfather had on Dunbar Street around 27th Avenue. "I don't even know his name, he was just my grandpa, my father's father: *gung* or *dai-gung*. He was the first one out to Canada, he worked, saved money, and brought his half-brothers out, my dad's uncles."

Larry remembers his *gung* as a strict old man who never betrayed any emotion. In the sales part of the store, it was always "Don't touch," and if he spied you fondling the fruit, you'd get a whack across the knuckles. "That's where you learned that the best fruit is for sale—you couldn't touch the number one fruit and vegetables."

His grandfather went back to his home village in China to die when Larry was still a young boy. He gave up the lease on the store, which he was renting; he hadn't bought it because there were both governmental and private restrictions limiting the property Chinese people could own back then.

Larry and his siblings shuttled between the reserve and Chinatown on the streetcar, the main form of public transit in Vancouver from the 1890s to the 1950s. They'd walk up to Dunbar and 41st Avenue from the reserve and catch the number 14 Hastings, which went down Dunbar, across Broadway to Granville, across the old Granville Street Bridge and all the way to Hastings; they'd get off at Hastings and Gore. It took about an hour and a half each way, sitting on wooden slat seats while the streetcar rattled along its tracks, powered by electric lines above. (The number 7 bus now follows the same route; the number 14 starts in Hastings but follows 10th Avenue to UBC. Both are still electric and use overhead wires, ghosts of the streetcars.)

"It travelled fairly good at that time because there was hardly any traffic," Larry says. "People mostly drove their cars on weekends; very, very few people drove to work back then, in the '40s. We'd go there to school sometimes during the week and then go back to the reserve on the weekend. Other times we'd just go daily on the streetcar from the reserve to school."

Of course, they weren't supposed to be living on the reserve, but as long as it wasn't their principal residence, and no one complained or told the Indian agent . . .

"How are you?" asks the server. We've just settled at a Formica table at Larry's regular diner, New Town Bakery and Restaurant on East Pender just west of Main Street, after pushing past the crowds at the door and the lone diners chowing down at the counter. The signs in the window feature photos of the most popular dishes, including dim sum specials and the "Best Steamed Buns in Town."

"I'm good," Larry replies. "Boys' day." He usually comes here with his wife.

"Do you know what you want? Take your time."

"What's the special today?"

"Every day is special. You want rice? House special on rice? Pork chop with rice? It's mixed meat with a little bit of seafood with liver. That OK?"

Larry explains that he usually has the house special. His wife has the pork chop, which is served with gravy and a lot of onions and rice. You have to ask if you need a knife; diners who are more skilled than he is with chopsticks pick it up with them and bite right into the meat.

He used to speak some Cantonese but understands very little these days. The four years doing evening classes at Chinese school were seventy-odd years ago now, and he never really spoke it much because the other Chinese kids at school never addressed him in Cantonese. "It was really challenging to speak Chinese, even then."

The server brings bowls of broth for us both and Larry says that the old restaurants all used to do that—serve you a bowl of broth to start off. Unless you ordered a big bowl of soup. Then everyone would eat out of it.

"My wife says I'm hard to cook for, I eat anything!" he adds. "If you grew up like me, food is food, you eat it. And you cooked it for me!"

As a kid he says he just ate a lot of mush. Eggs were a luxury; mostly it was rice, Chinese vegetables and, if you were lucky, some Chinese bacon or preserved duck. "The duck is like a little pancake, they steam it and steam and steam it. Just add spices, mostly ginger."

On the reserve it was different: clams, mussels, all the wild game that his papa (his Musqueam grandfather, Seymour; Dad was *baba*, a Chinese word) would bring, such as deer, geese, salmon, sturgeon, crabs. All seasonal food, like the Chinese. They got vegetables all summer long from the Chinese farmers, who grew two or even three crops a summer, unlike white farmers, who only grew one. They would preserve a lot of it too, for winter: pickled cabbage, dried and pickled bok choy. Mandarin oranges once a year, at Christmas; apples in the fall.

"We would sit and eat with Dad," Larry remembers. "You had to eat from every dish, had to put it in your mouth and eat it. You couldn't say, 'I don't think I like that.' He'd just reach out and put it in your bowl, because we all ate out of a bowl."

The server returns with two house specials: fish balls, fish, squid, barbecued pork, chicken, beef, liver and chicken gizzard, all in chicken broth with noodles and vegetables. There used to be pig stomach or tripe, *jay-too* in Chinese, but people don't appreciate that these days. "Too bad, I liked it," says Larry.

Back on the street, Larry is remembering a long-gone Chinese restaurant they frequented a few doors down. A couple of doors east was another place that served delicious apple tart and a Boston cream pie, fancy '40s food no one eats anymore. "BC

Royal, I think it was called. It was run by Chinese people; there's a Chinatown storytelling centre across there now."

Next door he points up to a wonderful old neon sign bolted to the second floor and held in place by cables. It reads "Sai Woo Chop Suey," the last two words in white on the belly of a smiling red, green and yellow rooster. Only the sign remains. "The original Sai Woo used to be kind of an exciting place to be in," Larry recalls, "because you could go downstairs. There was a dining room in the basement." Now it's Kosoo Pocha at Sai Woo, a "stylish spot in a heritage building [that] offers a shareable Asian fusion menu plus specialty cocktails," according to its website.

⁓⁓⁓⁓

"This here was a Texaco gas station. And this was a Chinese Presbyterian church."

We're a few metres to the north, at Gore and Pender, and Larry is laughing thinking about all the churches he found himself in as a kid: Catholic, Anglican, Presbyterian, Baptist, you name it. His mum used to make her children go on Sundays to the Catholic church on the reserve, but he always balked at contributing when the collection plate was passed around: "Our community was poor, we needed money for food."

In Chinatown, he went to Sunday school at the First United Church, because they gave out a little snack. "A white kid invited me. My mum encouraged me to go. I said, 'You know it's a mortal sin to go to another denomination?' She says, 'Well, no one will know. Go ahead and tell me what you learn.' She was a very spiritual woman, but not an organized church person, traditional but also accepting of Christian stories."

Then he learned that he could go to summer camp, and play baseball and soccer, as long as he kept going to Sunday school: "I found out they do everything the Catholics do but in a different way."

Then he discovered the Anglicans, St James' Anglican church. "Hey Mum, one of the kids at school says there's a boy scout group."

"Do you wanna go?"

"Well, I wanna see what it's about."

He attended about six cub meetings, where he learned all about the outdoors—"except I already knew all those things, that's exactly how we live at Musqueam. And now I'm Anglican!"

Another day, "Let's eat, we don't have any money, we can go to this mission, we'll sing and pray and then they'll feed us. The sermon was about the same guy." Jesus, our Saviour. The mission was on Water Street in Gastown, the oldest part of Vancouver.

Then he joined the Royal Canadian Air Force cadets. "Had to go to Memorial Day parade. 'All Roman Catholics step forward, you will go to Holy Rosary, rest go to Anglican,' they said. Next parade, I stepped forward—I wanted to see what would happen at Holy Rosary. I've always been like that."

Long and short, Larry guesses he's agnostic. "I believe in a higher power. I believe 90 percent of what we say at home, I've always been like that. I've always asked, 'Why do we believe in certain powers?' The how and why question is always strong in my mind. How come? 'Quit saying how come, that's just the way it is!' That's what my mum and aunties always said."

Larry got his beliefs from his grandparents, his aunties and his mother, stories of spirituality, how humans are connected to everything on the land. How they try to maintain all that through the medicines they've developed, through the generations that were here and must be remembered and honoured.

He was deeply moved the first time he went to a Sikh gathering and saw that they feed everyone, no questions asked. "That's humanity working, I'd never seen that. That I believe in."

Larry thinks the Christian religion has been used to dominate people all over the world, spoiling its original, radical philosophy. "They're not able to accept, from their doctrine, that other people have other ways of believing that they should respect. We believe that water, rocks, forest, trees, they all have a living force, a spirit. Stories connect all of that to people. When you go to Sunday school, you don't hear that. Paul feeding multitudes with his bucket of fish, that's a myth. If you heard that from an Indigenous person, you'd say, that can't be real, immediately. It's a magic trick."

/////////////

Back on Gore at Keefer, Larry is remembering that this was the back entrance to the beer parlour of a hotel. It's since been transformed into an apartment building. "The first time I'd ever seen my mother in a beer parlour," he says with a smile. "The sirens were going, horns were honking, people were crying and laughing: VE Day, May 8, 1945, the end of the war. Our dad dragged our mum in there, I remember them sitting there. Everyone was happy, going crazy, because the war was over. Singing, dancing. Even Mum, who doesn't drink!"

There used to be a lot of fights here when the pub shut down at eleven pm. Larry lived a few doors down in the Arno Rooms and would hear the shouting lying in bed. "A lot of Black people would fight at night, often with white people. Especially Saturday nights. You could hear the fights starting here, towards Hogan's Alley," the Black neighbourhood between Union and Prior that was bulldozed around 1970 to make way for a viaduct. "Sometimes they'd bounce against the window and you'd hope they didn't come through. A lot of guys got hurt."

"Was that scary, as a kid?"

"We were used to it," says Larry. "It was kind of like a Star Wars thing. You're scared, but you're excited."

Things didn't change much after the war ended. "There was a little bit of socializing that never happened otherwise, but then life went on."

Walking back to the car, Larry suddenly feels saddened at how Chinatown has changed. In the decades since he lived here, so many hubs of communal life have closed; he misses the sweet-smelling bakeries, the overflowing grocery stores, the steamy laundries, the huge restaurants with shared tables, even the gambling dens. The new places, the artisan cafés, are different; many of them are fancier, but they're not for families, they're for individuals, many sitting on their own communing with their phones or laptops.

The streets are not as crowded. We pass some elderly Chinese people, but hardly any parents or kids, and we don't hear Chinese being spoken as much as it was. "I know things evolve," Larry says, "but since the founding families that developed the place left, it's just not as dynamic. It's like a skeleton: no flesh, no life, no vibrancy."

And like the rest of the Downtown Eastside, it's really run-down. The pride is gone. What used to be a close-knit Chinese haven, a place to share and escape to and feel safe in, is becoming more and more like any other Canadian neighbourhood, a collection of individuals rather than a community.

At least he got some good sausage. His wife will be happy that he's making dinner tonight.

Chapter Four

Being Schooled /
Strathcona and Van Tech

"It was a good school," says Larry. "It had international students from around the world. Very mixed: Irish, Black, Japanese, Chinese, Italian. And a cafeteria—good hot lunch every day, for a quarter."

It's late June 2022, and Lord Strathcona, the largest and oldest school in Vancouver, has just closed its massive wooden doors for the year. Opened in 1891, it's an imposing complex of stone and brick buildings that takes up most of a city block in Vancouver's hardscrabble East End. For more than a century, it's provided classes from kindergarten to Grade 7 or 8 for some of the city's poorest children, many from immigrant families. It has always provided health and food programs as well, and now includes a library, community centre and dental clinic on site, plus the only all-day junior kindergarten in Vancouver.

Larry and his elder brother Gordon started school at Strathcona in 1941, when Larry was only five, and went there for the next nine years. Gordie was a strapping lad and always took care of his little brother physically, which was lucky, because Larry was small but lippy and fearless and didn't back down from fights.

"At that time, Strathcona was the centre of the immigrant area," Larry says. "You have the railways: the Great Northern, the Canadian National, the Burlington Northern coming into the Science World area, and the Canadian Pacific ships coming in. Immigrants got off the boat or train and they would live there until they earned enough money to move out. So you got to see all the different nationalities. That to me was a wonderful learning experience. At the time it was just a part of life, but then you reflect on it and see it was an enormous thing that happened. Learning about Chinese, Indigenous and immigrants from all over the world—it's quite an experience."

Part of that experience was being called an Indian for the first time. On the reserve the kids sometimes taunted him for being Chinese: "'Chinky Chinky Chinaman,' you know . . . Then you'd go downtown to Strathcona school and the parents of the children, and the children, would call us 'dirty Indians,' 'stinky smelly Indians.'"

In the ethnic hierarchy that dominated all interactions back then, the English (whose nickname was *Limeys*, a pretty mild insult) were at the top, with the Scots and Welsh just below them. The Irish were the third rung on the ladder. "At the very, very bottom, after the Italians and the Poles and the Russians and all the Orientals—I get called old-school for using that word, but it's the word they used back then—were the Indigenous people," recalls Larry. "And just a little bit above them were the Chinese."

In the schoolyard or the soccer field, every ethnic group had a nickname. Larry soon knew every racial slur, and used them when he had to, depending on the situation. "My friends were Polish, Ukrainian, Italian, Chinese, Japanese, Black, Irish, gypsies. We all knew the slang words we could call each other, though we didn't use them with ourselves. Except if we got into an argument, then we'd use them to retaliate."

In the classroom, the teachers—who were mostly English or Scottish—treated all the students equally. "We were very, very fortunate in that school," Larry says. "They all treated us with the same amount of respect, or disrespect, however you want to express it. They all said the same thing to us: 'Your brain's no bigger than my brain, my brain's no bigger than her brain, her brain's no bigger than yours. But we all have different wills.'"

"Like, willpower?"

"No, like, some will and some will not," he continues with a laugh. "And if you can't do that exercise, is it because you will not study? Do you think she gets an 'A' because she is smarter than you? She's not! She's more willing to do the work, that's what you have to do. That's how they treated us."

Indigenous children were not allowed to go to regular public schools at the time; until the federal law was amended in 1951, they were supposed to be in Indian residential school. Gordon and Larry slipped through the cracks by being Chinese, which turned out to be tricky because their father had entered Canada under a false name, which was printed on their ID. Luckily for them, the school gave them the benefit of the doubt and decided their surname was Hong, not Jang, their father's "paper" name.

Apart from his brother and sister, Larry only knew of one other Indigenous student, a boy whose father was non-status and lived off-reserve. Larry had always thought of himself as a mix, and though he looked Chinese, he felt more Musqueam because his mother had raised him in that culture. "She always maintained, quite vehemently, that, 'You are a Musqueam person, regardless of what people say to you. . . . You have

Cantonese blood in you, but you are a Musqueam person. You belong to Musqueam, and if you remember that in your life, you will be able to go anywhere and do whatever you want and you will always come home to Musqueam.'" That feeling of home was always in the back of his mind, a solace in all this racial turmoil.

When he moved on to the higher grades in school, Larry had differences with his history teacher and his homeroom teacher. When they told the class that the land had been empty before colonization because it wasn't used, he put up his hand and said, "No, my mother's people were here. For how many years I don't know, but they're not farmers—they're the Indian people. And the history doesn't show it correctly. Our people helped the newcomers in surviving."

"Well, it's not written down, so how can you say this?" the teacher asked.

"Because my mother told me all of this, and my mother doesn't lie," Larry replied. "She wouldn't lie about that."

//////////////

"This corner store was there back then," says Larry. He's looking in the tall window of Benny's Market at Union Street and Princess Avenue in Strathcona, Vancouver's East End. "It was a bit more expensive than the Chinese store. Probably still run by the same family."

A plaque in the window confirms this: the store was founded by and is still run by the Benedetti family, who emigrated from Abruzzo, Italy, in 1909. A faded sign from the Coca-Cola company says, "Italian Foods, celebrating Benny's 100th Anniversary." A sandwich board advertises the "Full Deli Inside: Hot and Cold

Sandwiches, Specialty Meats, Olives, Cheese & So Much More. Home of the Famous Benny Burger!"

The streets of Strathcona haven't changed much in the eight decades since Larry moved here in 1941. It's still an inner-city residential neighbourhood just east of Chinatown and south of Hastings Street, a grid of streets lined with brick and wooden bungalows, low-rise apartment buildings and housing projects. Many are stucco, and many have full-length porches; some apartment buildings have rusty fire escapes. Some houses are home to Chinese clan associations that aid new immigrants, like the Sam Duck Society at 462 Union, protected by metal bars and festooned with tattered flags in Chinese. Sirens wail and a fire truck roars past. The first responders ignore a junkie setting fire to a plastic bag in the alley, his green underwear showing above and through torn jeans.

"This is all new additions that replaced little houses," says Larry as we walk west along Union Street. Eighty years ago, Strathcona was mostly little houses, an endangered breed all over Vancouver these days, bulldozed to be replaced by monster homes or condo blocks. "There were always people sitting on the porch talking," Larry adds. "The wives would be at home, the mothers. And very little traffic. Mostly walking. Everybody used public transit and lived close to where they worked." Several streetcar lines met near here at Main and Hastings, including the number 14 that took Larry to 41st and Dunbar near the reserve.

"We live in such an artificial world now," Larry continues. "We don't know what it's like underneath, the farms, the earth. The young ones are not grounded to the land they come from, compared to when we were growing up. It's sad they don't experience that, it's all screens.

"A lot of our urban youth are disconnected from the knowledge of this interconnection and interdependency," Larry says. "They think land is off across the water, but it is right here. It is just covered and locked in by paved roadways, sidewalks and parking lots. The urban landscape works very hard to keep us disconnected from the deeper knowledge of the territory and its Indigenous inhabitants."

His thoughts return to the inner city in the 1940s. "We had bicycles. Racing across the old Georgia Viaduct downtown, the traffic was nothing. Riding from Main and Hastings back and forth on a bike was just normal, riding around Stanley Park, all over the waterfront."

Strathcona, the school and the neighbourhood, was a huge learning ground for social mores. On school grounds, you had to respect other people, and they had to respect you. Outside the school gates was a different world. "The Chinese fought the Italians, the Italians fought the Jews, the Jews fought the Blacks and the Blacks fought everybody," Larry says. "And then there were the Japanese . . ."

So soon after Pearl Harbor, the Japanese faced a lot of prejudice. "A couple of our best friends had spent their childhood up in Aspen Grove and Ashcroft, in the concentration camps that most of those kids in Strathcona were sent to," says Larry. "'Internment camps,' excuse me." From 1942 to 1949, Canada forcibly interned about twenty-two thousand Japanese Canadians, more than nine-tenths of the Japanese-Canadian population, in camps in the BC interior, after confiscating their possessions.

Back on Union Street, Larry is retracing his steps from school to Chinatown. "And the police, on the streets, although they don't do racial profiling," he says, shaking his head at the sarcasm. "My friends were a real mix: Irish, Black, Japanese, Chinese, Italian. If we were walking down the street together and somebody threw a rock at someone, it would be, 'You, you and you, get over here.' And it would be the children of colour. In school, we were all equal, but off school grounds, the racial thing just popped right up into the open."

Larry is writing this book in the hope that all our families and communities come to understand the hardships that many Canadians, especially Indigenous people, still live with today. "Hopefully it will get into the school system, so children that have been indoctrinated into white society privilege get to hear about their school mates of colour," he says. "Children of colour experience racism from birth, so non–people of colour should be able to accept and read about it. Children are very good at understanding fairness and equality."

Larry hopes to create meaningful dialogue and understanding between all of society, including those who have been colonized. "We need to get together to work towards equality and a more equitable understanding, so we can live and work together for a better life for the whole human race. That can only happen changing one mind at a time."

///////////

One night when he was about ten, at a movie on Granville Street downtown with some friends, Larry got whacked across the shoulders for refusing to stand and sing "God Save the King."

"Pretty strong young boy."

"Strong or stupid," he replies with a giggle. "I know how small I am. Theatre full of guys bigger than me, last movie is around midnight, and everybody stands up except me. I get a whack across the shoulders. 'Stand up for the king.'

"Not my king."

"Did you get away with that?"

"Slap across the back from behind. You stand up. Wrong time of night." But he'd made his point.

///////////////

During his early years at Strathcona, Larry and Gordon also went to Chinese school, "school after school." His father wanted them to learn how to read and write in Cantonese.

"This is the doorway that leads upstairs—the school was on the second floor," yells Larry. He's reached Pender Street at the corner of Gore Avenue and is looking up at a rundown old brick building with Hang Hing Herbal Medical Co. on the streetfront. A new six-storey condo building is going up across Gore, so he has to shout to be heard. Regular school ended at three o'clock and Chinese lessons ran from four 'til six, five days a week. The boys put up with this for three years until their father finally relented.

"Didn't really enjoy it because we didn't really speak it," Larry says. "We could understand it, but we never really spoke it. The majority of the kids were Chinese kids who could already speak it quite well—they were just learning how to read and write. Trying to catch up with them was quite challenging. It's really something because there's like six thousand characters or symbols." (There are in fact about fifty thousand, and they say you need to know at least three thousand to read the newspaper.)

"There used to be a gas station kitty corner to here," he adds.

"Where the organic cold-press juices are sold now?"

"Yep, right up to the alleyway. Next door is the same building."

"The Benevolence Society?"

"Yeah. The Chinese have a youth gathering there. Like a YMCA kind of thing."

///////////////

"This was a Chinese laundry. Right here." We've stopped on Union Street by the alley just east of Main. The building, modern and brick, is called The Union.

"One or two doors over is where I stayed when I started high school at Vancouver Tech. I lived with one of our father's distant relatives. Rented a room, me and my sister, who had just started Grade 9."

Most launderers back then were Chinese, but Larry never got his clothes washed by them—he would take his dirty laundry to the reserve.

"Did you do it or did your mum do it?"

"Kind of half and half. London Drugs was on the other side here, when London owned it. A Jewish family."

"Was their name London?"

"Yes. H.Y. Louie bought it and expanded it from here.

"In this same area, Prior Street, was Vie's Chicken and Steak House, run by a Black woman. That was a very famous spot. People went there after hours, during the evening. You'd have a steak and bring your own bottle under the table."

Larry was at Strathcona school one year longer than he should have been, because he caught rheumatic fever during Grade 2 and ended up missing a whole year. He finally finished Grade 8 and graduated in 1951, aged fourteen, and started that fall at Vancouver Technical High School.

The first and best vocational school in British Columbia, Van Tech is still housed in an imposing yellow building on East

Broadway in the city's East End. It had impressive workshops and laboratories where the students (mostly boys; it only welcomed girls in 1940) were given rigorous practical training for a career in the trades.

Larry says he was lucky to get to high school at all; he reckons about 30 percent of the boys at Strathcona never went beyond Grade 8. "We had to go to work. Then in high school, the instructors used to say, 'Somebody comes along and offers you a job—a high-paying job with good conditions—you should go. Finish your schooling later. Go. Because a work opportunity only comes once.'" No wonder so many children of immigrants didn't complete their education.

The training he got at Van Tech was excellent: a lot of theory, a lot of hands-on. In Grade 9 he did every kind of shop: sheet metal, drafting, electrical. Grade 10 was foundry and welding, and some machine shop: "We did a little bit, not much. They wouldn't let you in too much. But you had four years of laughing."

Then he started his concentration, mechanics, training in the machine shop and the mechanic shop. He also chose an elective: woodwork. "Not machines," he says. "I didn't care too much for being a machinist. I liked it, but I wanted to work on heavy-duty equipment in a factory. They were just coming in. Highly skilled work."

All the work was monitored and had to be very precise. He learned all the skills you would need to work in an automotive machine shop: pin fitting, cylinder boring, repairing valves, surface grinding. He mastered a little thirty-inch lathe that no one else really used and learned how to repair cracked cast iron without welding.

It took years for Larry to fully realize how much he'd learned at Van Tech. There was a stationary engineering program there, and a huge, six-cylinder diesel engine they could work on. "Must have been the size of a locomotive," he says. "Bigger than a locomotive engine because you had a ladder to get to the top of it."

BCIT (the British Columbia Institute of Technology) hadn't been created yet, so Larry did his apprenticeship theory classes at night school at the Vancouver Vocational Institute (now Vancouver Community College) at Pender and Cambie streets downtown. They didn't have a program for automotive machinists and didn't know what to do with Larry and the one other apprentice, Ray Hunt, so they were put in the automotive class.

"My friend and I had gone to Van Tech together and he said, 'We've done all this. Let's ask them if we can challenge it.'"

Larry replied, "Well, you ask them because they won't listen to me. They'll listen to you because you're white."

The two boys challenged and passed the first year in automotive and got into second year—only to discover that they'd learned all of it at Van Tech too. So they challenged that year also. Ditto third year. At which point the authorities put their foot down; Larry and Ray were told, "We cannot give you certification in less than four years." So they spent four years doing any training they could find in the shop, showing up just to put in the time. Larry studied automatic transmissions and differential and automotive electric.

By then he was working eight to five as an indentured apprentice, with M&M Motor Parts. "I don't know if they still exist today," he says, "but their partner does, Pacific Parts. I took up woodwork also. Learned how to make furniture and stuff, how to work very precisely with wood."

So why didn't Larry go to university? Van Tech had three programs: high school graduation, general; university entrance; and trades entrance. Larry had all the credits he needed to go into the university entrance program; the only difference with the trades program at that time was the language requirement: French, German or Spanish.

Two things made him choose trades. First of all, being very cash-poor, no one in his family had ever finished high school before him; both Gordon and Helen dropped out after Grade 9 or 10. His younger brother, Howard, would go on to study at Langara College (now University), the first family member to get any post-secondary education, but that was years away; he was still in elementary school when Larry was in Grade 12.

Second, when he thought of university, Larry imagined structural engineering or infrastructure work of some kind. But knowing that Chinese people were not allowed in the professions, could never be admitted as engineers or teachers, made that a non-starter. Why spend years studying and not be able to get a job at the end of it?

The next best thing was being an automotive mechanic or machinist, the only apprenticeship on offer when he graduated.

Looking back, Larry realizes he was lucky to get out of Strathcona and Van Tech in one piece. His refusal to gamble or do drugs, influenced by his mother and in reaction to his father's addictions, probably helped. "I bet you by the time I graduated from high school in '55 over half of those kids I went to school with in Strathcona, the immigrant kids, were dead or in jail," he says. "Gangs, violence, drugs—and the drug of choice at that time was heroin."

By the time he started at Van Tech, Larry was mostly living in Musqueam, and by Grade 10, he had moved back to the float-house permanently. His grandparents had passed on by then, so he shared the cramped space with his mother and his three siblings, doing his homework on a little kitchen dinette table lit by a kerosene lamp, the light flickering out across the massive dark river. The only heat came from a wood-burning stove that doubled as a kitchen range; the only sounds were the waves sloshing beneath their feet and the birds twittering all around. "No white noise!" says Larry with a smile. It was damp but warm, a loving space that still evokes strong feelings of family and home.

"That's probably the place we really enjoyed the most, the place with the fondest memories, although it was tiny," Larry says. "It was *very* dark. Once the sun went down there was no light except maybe the lamp and the starlight or the moonlight," reflecting off the blue-black river. Larry would draw the curtain when his mum had visitors, to keep warm and get a little privacy. The only entertainment was a radio, and they were so poor they could only listen to it one or two hours a day, because batteries were expensive.

"A couple of the guys I went to Strathcona with who were at Van Tech asked, 'Hey, why don't you invite us out to your place? You're always at our place.' I said, 'OK, catch the number 14 on Hastings Street and take it all the way to the end of the line. Walk down. There's only one road, it's dirt—just follow the wagon tracks. It's about a mile walk.'"

When they arrived, his friends said, "Holy cow. We thought you were fooling. You do live in a little place, and you don't have electricity."

He replied, "The toilet's out there. You see that little shack over there? It's a three-holer. One of the old original, multi-bathroomed homes!"

The water was in a standpipe, a vertical pipe connecting a temporary tap to the main. There were about five standpipes by the river, and in the winter they would freeze. The boys thought he lived in the country because the walk down passed through a few hundred metres of forest, an eerie, otherworldly remnant of Vancouver's original wilderness.

"The whole atmospheric dynamic is quite different still," says Larry. "People who come down and visit all say the same thing: 'It's so quiet.' Birds chirping. But it's real noisy for me today. It was very quiet when I was a kid."

Larry's grandfather had tied the floathouse high up on the beach so that the front end of the logs only floated at high tide. But the back end of the house was on the slope of the beach, so when the tide went down the back was higher than the front—and twice a day, at high tide, the house would level out.

Larry laughs thinking about it now. "And at low tide the back of the house would maybe be a foot lower than the front!"

Chapter Five

The School Larry *Didn't* Go To /
In Mission City

The Fraser River Heritage Park in Mission city doesn't look like a crime scene. The lush, hilly park an hour's drive east of Vancouver on the Lougheed Highway is a beautiful spot popular with locals, who walk their dogs along the gravel pathways and picnic in the white, eight-sided gazebo. Afterwards they may have a latté on the dog-friendly patio of the Blackberry Kitchen, a white-linen coffee shop and restaurant with spectacular views of the flat, fertile Fraser Valley to the south and beyond to Washington state, where the snowy, glacier-covered peak of the volcano Mount Baker dominates the horizon.

On this cold, sunny day in February, Larry is walking fast to keep warm. He's come to remember his many cousins and friends who were sent to St. Mary's residential school in Mission, eighty kilometres due east of Musqueam Reserve No. 2, but we're having a hard time finding the remains of the original Catholic school, run by the Oblates of Mary Immaculate; the imposing brick buildings were demolished in 1965, four years after a new, federal-run residential school had opened next door. They are in the park somewhere, but we can't find a sign telling us where. It should be marked; after all, the city was named after the Catholic mission that ran the school for over a century.

The first remnant we find is the original bell, housed in an elegant new wooden bell tower. A sign explains that it was cast in West Troy, New York, in 1875 and rang to signal class and mealtimes until the old school was torn down, when it was moved to the new St. Mary's. In 1999, the Stó:lō Nation—the Musqueam's hənq̓əminəm̓-speaking relatives from the Fraser Valley—donated it to the park, where it's now on display.

Then Larry sees a sunken, rectangular grassy patch partly covered by dry leaves next to the bell tower. A small brass plaque on one side reads, "Boys' Dormitory / Mission House / Built 1884." No other trace remains of this structure. But on the other side of the rhododendron garden next to it we spy another sunken, stone-lined rectangle filled with grass and leaves. A collection of children's shoes, six tiny pairs, is lined up neatly along the remains of a low stone wall on the far side. A second plaque here reads, "Girls' Dormitory." Verdant with moss and grass in the crisp winter air, the scene is unbearably poignant.

Neither of us can speak; ghosts haunt this place. The souls of little girls and boys, forcibly separated from their families and brought to this cold, loveless place to have the "Indian" driven out of them.

At last, half hidden under a low tree, we find a weathered sign explaining that this is indeed the site of the former St. Mary's Indian Residential School. "The foundations of the old buildings are all that remain of the School, which operated in this location from 1882 until the opening of the new school in 1961," it reads. The first Catholic school opened down by the river in 1863, but was moved up here to make room for the Canadian Pacific

Railway tracks twenty years later. When the new federal school closed in 1984, it was the last functioning residential school in British Columbia. About two thousand students attended its various iterations during its 121-year history, mostly from Stó:lō but also from further afield, including many from Musqueam and others from as far north as Lillooet in the Fraser Canyon.

"The original interpretive signs were removed by the City of Mission," the sign continues, "as they did not adequately reflect the story of St. Mary's, nor did they reflect our deeper understanding of the long-term impacts of the residential school system, enacted by the Government of Canada. A small group of First Nations representatives are engaging with the City and have commenced discussions to develop new signs or interpretive elements, to further educate the community and reflect on the devastating impact of the residential school systems and the long-term harm caused to so many."

The sign ends with a plea for understanding, in large letters at the bottom:

"We appreciate your patience as the work continues."

Patience indeed, Larry thinks, shaking his head. We can only guess how long those discussions have been going on. The sign is ancient and barely legible, its plastic coating badly damaged by the rain.

A jogger cruises by, the tinny sound of his music breaking the silence.

Just to the east of the girls' dormitory is the Oblates of Mary Immaculate cemetery, where priests, nuns and students from the mission and its school were buried starting in 1870. A photo from 1958 shows at least twelve graves outside the high metal fence that surrounds it, an area now covered by blackberry bushes and strewn with iron-cross grave markers. In 2021, after the discovery of more than two hundred unmarked graves at a residential school site in Kamloops made news around the world, the Stó:lō Nation announced that they would be examining this site for unmarked graves, combining modern technology such as ground-penetrating radar with testimony from Elders who attended the school or brought their children here.

Surrendering to the cold, we head to the Blackberry Kitchen for coffee and a cinnamon bun.

/////////////

"Canada's residential school system for Aboriginal children was an education system in name only for much of its existence." So begins the final report of the Canadian Truth and Reconciliation Commission (TRC), an eight-year investigation into the legacy of the country's residential school system. "These residential schools were created for the purpose of separating Aboriginal children from their families," it continues, "in order to minimize and weaken family ties and cultural linkages, and to indoctrinate children into a new culture—the culture of the legally dominant Euro-Christian Canadian society."

Between 2008 and 2014, the TRC collected testimonies from more than six thousand witnesses from across Canada. Its final report estimated that around 150,000 children attended the schools during their 120-year history, and many were abused and neglected. It concluded that the policy amounted to cultural genocide.

So what is reconciliation, exactly? The TRC grappled with this question and concluded that the concept meant different things to different people, communities, organizations and institutions—notably the various First Nations, the federal government and the churches who ran most of the schools. They also agreed that it is an ongoing process that will require a lot of work and commitment from all those affected by it; not just directly but indirectly, including *all* Canadians.

"Aboriginal or non-Aboriginal Canadians from all walks of life spoke to us about the importance of reaching out to one another in ways that create hope for a better future. Whether one is First Nations, Inuit, Métis, a descendant of European settlers, a member of a minority group . . . or a new Canadian, we all inherit both the benefits and obligations of Canada. We are all Treaty people who share responsibility for taking action on reconciliation."

In their final report, the commission also warned against the rush to reconciliation. Like any grieving process, it has steps, none of which can be skipped. The first of these, begun by the TRC in its cross-country hearings, is truth-telling. Next come justice and healing. Only then can true reconciliation begin.

"Go slow, we are going too fast," one residential school survivor told the commission. "We have many tears to shed before we even get to the word reconciliation."

///////////////

At the top of the road leading to the school, Larry stops abruptly and says, "We used to come here to visit."

"Visit?"

"Yeah, once a year or something, whenever we could scrounge up a vehicle. We'd drive up here and end up smack in the middle between the girls' dorm and the boys' dorm. We'd try and see one of our cousins in the window and wave. 'See you guys!' That's as close as you could get."

Every year, some of Larry's many friends and cousins, all the kids he'd grown up playing with on the reserve, were sent off to residential school. Most came here, though a few went to other, similar schools: St. Augustine's in Sechelt, on the Sunshine Coast; St. Paul's in North Vancouver; Coqualeetza, a Protestant school in Chilliwack, forty kilometres east of Mission; Alberni, near Port Alberni on Vancouver Island.

Because he was so young when all this started, it took Larry a long time to understand what was going on. But he and his siblings missed their playmates, so their aunts and uncles drove them here to try and catch a sight of their children through the windows; no visits were allowed, and some kids didn't come home for Christmas or the summer.

After these fleeting visits, Larry's aunts and uncles would take all the visitors to the Mission city store to get a bottle of pop.

"Long way to come for a pop."

"It was a road trip and if we were lucky, we'd get to see our cousins. That was the real trip, to see our cousins."

A few years later, when his big brother Gordie could drive, the brothers and another band member, Vern, "borrowed" a pickup truck and came to visit the cousins on their own. Word got around that there were some guys out there, on a visit. The boys were saying, "Hey, there's Nita, there's Johnny." Someone waved. Then a monitor shooed them away. "There was always some monitor on hand, to make sure they didn't jump out the window," says Larry. "You couldn't visit, couldn't get close and talk. At least you got the wave."

"If the reserve was a minimum-security prison," he adds, "residential school was maximum-security."

Only now does any of this forced separation make any sense. "They were sent here because they were 'Indian,'" Larry says. "We weren't taken, because we were 'Chinese.'"

In truth, Larry and his siblings were mixed heritage. They were far from unique in this on the reserve; many of his friends and cousins had diverse roots. In fact, his mother and her two sisters all married outside Musqueam. "Three different daughters, three different husbands, three different nationalities," he says. "A Chinese one, an Indian one, and a Norwegian one. My grandfather used to say to my mother, 'I really want to see how my grandchildren turn out—which one's going to be a Musqueam person?' And it was the Chinese kids." In retrospect he sees that's probably because they didn't go to residential school, and thus had closer ties to their mother's family.

At the time, Larry was sad about being left behind—he wanted to be with his friends and cousins! But then he started to hear the stories about St. Mary's. Brothers and sisters were separated, and didn't see their parents or other family members for months or years on end. Recollections and experiences varied, but conditions seemed to get worse with the years. Many students were physically and sexually abused, with the Indian Residential School Survivors Society describing the abuse at St. Mary's in the 1960s as "nightmarish."

Years later Larry learned that the priest on the reserve who had warned his mother about this place was right—the "school" didn't bother much with education. The students were lonely, malnourished and exhausted, and spent most of their time and energy working in the dairy farm, the laundry or the bakery rather than studying. They were always hungry and told stories of crawling through the basement windows to steal potatoes or apples from the underground storage rooms. They learned very little, except how to survive—and that they were stupid and Indigenous culture was inferior to white, Christian culture.

Larry's cousins would talk about the different means of punishment, the isolation, the physical and mental abuse. "As a child, we didn't think much of it," Larry says. "It doesn't sink in. But then you realize what a saving grace being half Chinese was."

Larry has come to see that he wasn't just fortunate because he escaped the abuse and the attacks on his self-worth—he's also fortunate because, unlike his cousins, he grew up socializing with the older generation, living every day in the heart of a loving community. "What was it like to welcome a new baby? To go to a wedding or a funeral in the Big House? Those were the things we got to experience."

He and his siblings were sometimes the only children of school age in any community or gathering, so they became everyone's toys and playthings. "We were the ones that got taken for ice cream and candy and hugged," he says. "Wondering why you got a hug. You don't even know that lady."

"That's fascinating. I never thought about it that way."

"That's what I'm saying. Nobody talks about the parents that got left behind. The parents' generation. And the little kids, the three-year-olds; they'd go, 'Where's my brother? Where's my sister?'"

For the parents and grandparents, losing a child to residential school was like a death in the family. "'My kids are gone. Where are they?'" Larry asks. "You know where they are, but you can't go visit them. And when they come out, they don't belong anymore. Can't figure out how to belong. Maybe can't even exist with their cultural practices."

He's thought a lot about the parents and grandparents who lost their children and grandchildren. What did they do? What were their lives like? What do you live for? "You want to see your grandkids and show them the things you know," Larry says. "But you can't do that. And when those kids come home, will they accept what you know? They don't know how to be Indigenous anymore." They were suspicious of Indigenous culture, of their own parents and siblings and cousins.

The older people on the reserve used to sometimes mention that Larry and his siblings had more advantages than their children did, because they were at home with their mother and their grandparents all year long. In his younger days, Larry didn't give that much thought. "But then the first residential school episode came out publicly"—in the late 1990s—"and then everything started to make sense. We did have an advantage. We went to a public school that treated us like we were just regular kids. And we also saw our grandparents working, doing cultural things, nurturing each other and just being good people, in the sense that they were able to adapt to life situations and deal with that, while a lot of our cousins couldn't." Only then did Larry start to realize that he had a really rich cultural background and was very lucky to have not been robbed of it.

He compares residential school to the ongoing foster children policy: "White people who foster an Indigenous child—that's assimilation. The government says it's for the benefit of the child, the safety of the child. Then the kid ages out and you kick him out of the house. 'I don't get any money for you anymore; I'm not responsible for you anymore.' Off you go; you're on your own.

There's no support services like for kids who stay with their parents until they're twenty-five years old. Assimilation policy." Both foster kids and residential school kids have no culture, no home to hurry back to when they need consoling—it's a transaction, and then it's over and they're thrust out into an uncaring world, alienated and alone. No wonder so many end up on the streets, lost, on drugs, with no direction home.

"The residential school system was created to kill the Indian in the child, to remove all vestiges of Indian culture out of that child," Larry says. "And what it did was break up families. Children were kidnapped, basically, and forcibly taken to the Indian residential schools, to be away from their parents, from their language, and all other community members. It's a completely disconnected child that comes out of that school. Disconnected from self-worth, from community, from family, culture, spirituality, geography."

People who are disconnected from all that will begin to self-medicate. And if you have no self-worth, where do you go? To addiction: addiction to work, addiction to sex, addiction to drugs, addiction to gambling.

"Or because I am worthless, I don't belong to anything, what is life worth?" Larry continues. "Commit suicide."

Standing by the remains of the girls' dormitory, Larry raises his arms in anger. "My cousins were told by the sisters and monks and priests, here at St. Mary's at Mission, that they wouldn't amount to anything. Their self-worth was destroyed."

One of his cousins, who Larry had encouraged to go into an apprenticeship, told him, "I don't know how to do that, I'm not smart enough. I don't have the brains." And yet he was capable of taking an engine apart and putting it back together. He could wire a house, do all sorts of trade work. But he kept insisting, "I'm not as smart as you, cousin."

"And you know why he thought that?" asks Larry. "'You're that smart because you're half Chinese and I'm not, I'm just Indian. So I can't do those things.' That's what he'd been taught. That's how deep it goes."

Many of his cousins committed suicide, each in their own way. Some by drinking, others by drugs or other forms of neglect or self-abuse or addiction. Two hanged themselves.

The more Larry thinks about St. Mary's, the angrier he gets. "I think of those cousins who aren't here anymore, who were ten, fifteen years younger than me. Growing up they were just part of our lives. All of these legislated acts, how cruel they were, how they dehumanized people so they could do things that were really crimes against humanity. The abuse. The neglect.

"Those are the kind of emotions that come out now."

In 2002, investigations led by an RCMP task force led to thirteen people being charged of crimes against children at residential schools in British Columbia. The group looked into nearly a thousand separate allegations of physical and sexual abuse at fifteen schools. One of the people found guilty was a seventy-eight-year-old monk living in a monastery in Saskatchewan; he was convicted of twelve counts of indecent assault of young boys at St. Mary's school in the 1950s and '60s and sentenced to three years in prison. Several other employees were investigated but not charged.

///////////

The Canadian Truth and Reconciliation Commission ended with ninety-four "Calls to Action" to "redress the legacy of residential schools and advance the process of Canadian reconciliation." Many of these focus on education, because non-Indigenous Canadians still find it hard to accept that such widespread and systemic abuses, in the words of the TRC report, "could have happened in a country such as Canada, which has long prided itself on being a bastion of democracy, peace, and kindness throughout the world."

In its report, the commissioners talk about the importance of Canadians from all walks of life reaching out to each other in ways that create hope for a better future. A noble aim, but what form does reconciliation take? The divide between settlers and Indigenous people is deep. The authors of this book see their unlikely, meandering conversations as one small part of this vast, decades-long process of talking and—the hard part for settlers—shutting up and really listening. "To hear what they are listening to," says Larry.

Growing up in Prince George in central British Columbia, my high-school year was one of the first to include Indigenous students. Children from the Nadleh Whut'en First Nation had previously been sent to the notorious Lejac residential school in nearby Fraser Lake, but after it closed in 1976, the city's high schools became integrated for the first time; like St. Mary's in Mission, Lejac was razed to the ground soon afterwards. But Social Studies 11, the Canadian history class Indigenous and non-Indigenous students alike had to take, contained no mention of residential schools; it covered Confederation and the building of the railroad, with a recognition of the role of Chinese labour, but other than Métis leader Louis Riel, Indigenous people barely got a look in. (In Larry's eyes, "The CPR railroad and stations are this country's biggest monument to slavery and disrespect of the lives of people of colour.")

The TRC's Calls to Action 62–65: Education for Reconciliation has changed that. My seventeen-year-old son Sami will be part of the second high-school class in British Columbia that has to take at least one Indigenous-focused course to graduate; he's signed up for Social Studies 12: Contemporary Indigenous Issues.

"What's the course called again?" asks Larry.

"Contemporary Indigenous Issues."

"They're all contemporary. There are no issues that are defunct. Whatever we were arguing over as children, we are still arguing about here today. With a different audience. But it's happening, there's a curriculum being developed, Indigenous activists are busy, they're in the forefront."

None of this is ancient history; it's all within living memory. St. Mary's closed in 1984, the last and longest-running residential school in BC; several others in other provinces were still running into the late 1990s. As William Faulkner wrote in *Requiem for a Nun*, "The past is never dead. It's not even past."

Larry adds that it's a sad thing, in this country of freedom and democracy, that it took the courts to make any of this happen.

"Truth and reconciliation were decreed by the court?"

"Yes—TRC was a court case. Murray Sinclair, an ex-judge, headed it. Then all the recommendations were brought forward through a court decree. It's not the federal government, it's a federal, court-ordered decree that opened the doors to this massive search for information from First Nations people. All of a sudden it's the law of the land, and everyone is asking for information. 'We have to follow the Calls to Action.' It's crazy that that's what it takes."

The UN Declaration on the Rights of Indigenous Peoples, which took almost three decades to create, is similar; it was announced in 2007, adopted by Canada in 2021, and passed into law by British Columbia in January 2024, in a groundbreaking precedent noted worldwide.

The next generation will have the chance to reckon with and atone for past wrongs. Maybe they will be the ones to write those new signs in Fraser River Heritage Park the Stó:lō and Musqueam have been waiting patiently for all these years.

All this will come way too late for Larry's cousins.

⁂

Is there bitterness in the Musqueam community that this process of truth, justice, healing and reconciliation has taken so long to get going?

"It's been a challenge," Larry says diplomatically. "It's a sensitive thing to talk about, and if nothing's going to happen, you have to let it go. Not forget it, but not let it eat away at you. That's the challenging part.

"When I talk, do a lecture or something, they say, 'You don't sound bitter.' I say, 'Well you should see it from this side. I am bitter. But if I come across to you as very bitter, you're not going to listen to me, you'll feel defensive. Either that or all of a sudden you'll get guilty about something you shouldn't have to, and you won't listen to my story.'

"And that's so important—for you to listen to my story, to really hear what I am saying."

But how does he do that, inside himself? How do you get past the bitterness?

"It's not easy. At times it'll come out when you're talking, and you'll say to yourself, 'Oh no, don't do that!'"

The February sun is setting behind the high mountains to the south of Fraser River Heritage Park, painting it with orange light. The dog walkers have gone home and the air is even chillier. The tattered sign appreciating our patience flaps in the wind. So do the dry leaves in the foundations of the school dormitories, barely visible in the twilight except for the six tiny shoes decorating one wall.

Chapter Six

The Longshoreman Years /
On the Vancouver Docks

On a cold winter's day, the glaciers on the high peaks above Chilliwack sparkle like distant gemstones in the bright sunshine. The steep, rocky faces of the Cascade range, dominated by mounts Cheam and Slesse, tower over the lush green farmland below, divided up by arrow-straight roads and wandering sluice ditches, all flat as a tabletop.

"Beautiful, eh?"

"Oh yeah," Larry replies. "But it's only February—should be like that in June. Used to be all white at this time of year, middle of winter. A little bit of snow like that, it's more like June."

The spectacular mountain vista at the eastern end of the Fraser Valley has reminded Larry of a trip he made up there long ago, when he was sixteen or seventeen and driving a three-ton truck between Vancouver and the Chilliwack area, picking up berries and fruit from local farmers. Some of the farms were in Rosedale, right across the river from Agassiz, where Larry was born. "Just before Bridal Falls, where the ferry across the river used to be," he says.

Every now and then, Larry and his boss would drive up the winding roads of Chilliwack Mountain to collect blackberries from the Mennonites who farmed and lived up there. The views west across the valley to the Pacific and Vancouver Island beyond were spectacular. And though drinking alcohol was against their religion, the farmers made their own blackberry wine and would always offer visitors a drink after the truck was loaded.

"The Hutterites and Mennonites, they don't drink but they had great wine," Larry says.

"What would they do with it, sell it?"

"I don't think so—somehow it would evaporate," he says with a sly smile. "I remember being up there, the boss man was driving the truck and I was his swamper, helper. The old man we were getting blackberries from said, 'You want a taste of wine?' My boss said sure—but not him. He's under twenty-one."

Larry has worked his whole life. By age eleven he was helping his dad and his uncles on the family farm on the reserve, toiling in the fields weeding and harvesting vegetables. At thirteen he got his first outside job, after school as a gas jockey at the Shell station at Georgia and Gore downtown. "We literally pumped gas," he says, "because we had to pump it out of the underground tanks." He makes a back-and-forth gesture with his arm, bending at the elbow. "Fill up that glass container of gasoline, it was marked off in half gallons."

As soon as he got his driver's licence, he got a better-paid job, the one that took him to Chilliwack Mountain: driving trucks in the summer while he was still at school. "Never did get a taste of blackberry wine, but it sure smelt good! The boss man didn't want me to have any, so that's fine."

When he graduated from high school in 1955, Larry was set on becoming an automotive mechanic: a car specialist. But the postwar economy was in a downturn at the time, and there were no automotive or heavy-duty mechanic apprenticeships on offer in Vancouver. The closest ones were in Prince George, eight hundred kilometres north, or on the construction site of the Peace River Dam, four hundred kilometres farther north near the border with Alberta, learning the trade with Caterpillar on their heavy machinery. "Being a scaredy-cat, I was afraid to leave Vancouver in '55, fresh out of high school," Larry says.

So he took the only job he could get, working as a shipping clerk in the basement of Black Brothers, at Hornby and Davie streets downtown. "It's a health spa right now," Larry says with a laugh. "It used to be an automotive parts house." It was boring, low-paid work with no future, but he needed a job to survive.

Luckily a friend from high school saw him there one day and said, "What are you doing in here? Ya want an apprenticeship?"

"Yeah, sure do," Larry replied. "Is there one available?"

"Yeah, automotive machinist," his friend replied. "Better than this! I'll get you that contact and a phone number, and you come out and be a machinist."

In high school Larry had disliked machinist work because it was very intense. When he told the instructor he wanted to be a mechanic, the man said, "Why don't you drop the automotive program and major in machine shop? You're excellent at it. A mechanic is just a machinist with his brains knocked out!" As fate would have it, he did end up apprenticing to become an automotive machinist, and truly appreciated it. He spent the next eleven years rebuilding engines, transmissions and rear ends, which was basically automotive work, but to a finer degree than a maintenance mechanic would have done it.

"And true to his word I did excel," says Larry. "But that's just my personal opinion."

Larry did his apprenticeship and then worked for just over a decade at M&M Motor Parts, at 5th Avenue and Manitoba, in the light-industrial area between Main and Cambie that is now home to many tech start-ups and craft breweries. As an automotive machinist, he re-machined every part of piston-driven gasoline engines, reboring cylinders, grinding crankshafts, repairing valves, pin fitting; "any kind of honing that requires accurate fitting." He found that truck engines were not much bigger or more complex than car engines. About the only engines he didn't work on were large train locomotives, which had to be sent to Alberta.

When he decided he was old enough to own his own vehicle, Larry discovered that living on the reserve came with its limitations. He knew the manager at the Bank of Nova Scotia, where he cashed his paycheque every two weeks. So he went in one day and told the man he needed to borrow nine hundred dollars to buy a car.

"Sure, I know you, Larry, no problem," came the reply. "What's your address?"

Larry gave him his postbox number.

"OK, that's the post office, but where do you live?"

"On the Musqueam reserve."

"OK, sorry, we can't give you a loan." Apparently it was a rule across Canada; people living on reserves couldn't own land or property and thus had no collateral, in the event they defaulted on their payments.

"Sorry, Larry, it's just a rule. We can't seize your assets, so we can't loan you money."

So for another few years, Larry lived in the floathouse on the reserve and took the trolley bus to work.

///////////

In 1966, when he was thirty years old, Larry lost his job in the machine shop. Luckily he had a backup plan.

His first father-in-law, Francis, looked after fishing boats for BC Packers, a conglomerate that ran fish canneries all over British Columbia, including a number along the Fraser River. When Larry became an automotive machinist, Francis knew he could rebuild engines and asked his son-in-law to look after the boats. So Larry started doing that on the side while he was working at M&M.

"I was still an automotive machinist, but I was doing this stuff on weekends because I needed the money, working two jobs basically," he says. When he got laid off at the machine shop, his father-in-law suggested he go down to the BC Packers head office in Vancouver to see if they had any work. He talked to the man in charge of the northern divisions, who hired him on the spot.

"You've been working on Francis's boats?"

"Yup, I'm the one."

"OK. Tomorrow you fly out to Prince Rupert."

Rupert, as the locals call it, is a town halfway to Alaska on British Columbia's Central Coast. It's famous for its rain, but Larry liked it. "It reminded me of the Vancouver of my childhood: the little houses; the jewellery stores; David Spencer, the department store." This was also his first plane ride, on a DC-3 or DC-4. Everybody said, pack your rain gear, it rains. But the whole month of June was sunny, not a drop. Then it started raining, intense sideways rain, every day after that. Sometimes only for a few minutes, but every goddam day.

The job was at Sunnyside Cannery, part of British Columbia's "Cannery Row," a remote collection of salmon canneries strung along Inverness Passage just south of Prince Rupert at the mouth of the Skeena, the province's second biggest river after the Fraser. For millennia, the Tsimshian and Gitxsan First Nations had lived off the huge salmon runs here, and since the mid-1800s, seasonal canneries had exploited them; at the turn of the century there were dozens of canneries there, processing tens of thousands of salmon for shipping in tins around the world.

The employees there and on the fishing boats were mostly Chinese, Japanese, Tsimshian and Gitxsan. They worked long hours for low wages and lived on site in makeshift accommodation perched precariously on wooden stilts or rocky beaches by the wild Pacific, on the edge of the dense coniferous forest. (When tourism replaced fishing as the main industry, the coast to the south was renamed The Great Bear Rainforest.) "They had the Chinese bunkhouse where all the Chinese ate and lived, in little rooms smaller than prison cells," says Larry. "Then they had a Japanese bunkhouse, and then downriver you had the Aboriginal camp. Everybody was segregated, even between administration and trades."

But Larry was hired as a shore boat mechanic, which meant first-class facilities. "I got to go into the main bunkhouse, with the white guys," he says in an ominous tone.

One of them, a young, red-haired boat carpenter nicknamed "Woodpecker," wasn't happy when he heard his new roommate was Chinese. When he was assigned to his room, Larry saw two empty beds there. At supper that evening, he asked the boss who his bunkmate was. The man pointed Woodpecker out, so Larry went over to speak to him, only to be told, "Fuck off, I'm not sleepin' with no slant-eyed, chopstick-wielding person!"

"What are you talking about?" Larry replied.

"My uncle died in Hong Kong" was the answer.

"That was the Japanese, what's that got to do with me?" Larry replied.

"Well, you're slant-eyed."

"Well, yeah," Larry said. "What's that got to do with anything? I wasn't in that war; I didn't kill him. You know how many of my Aboriginal relatives are still in Europe? Buried over there because they wanted to fight for Canada in the Second World War, and some in the First? You think I'm angry at the German people? I'm not. You think I'm angry at the Japanese people? I'm not. I'm here to make a living, and that's all I'm here for."

Before the end of the summer, Woodpecker had become Larry's buddy. After about six weeks, he came up to Larry and said, "Hey, Chopsticks"—Larry laughs a little at this memory; by then everyone was calling him that—"I apologize for what I said."

To which Larry replied, "Well, there's no need to apologize because you're ignorant." (He laughs again remembering that and adds, "He almost got upset at me again! Well, he was ignorant; ignorant of the facts.")

"No," replied Woodpecker. "But I know now that you're not the guy I thought you were. And you're a hell of a good mechanic."

"Yeah, I know I am," said Larry. "I know how good I am."

In that type of employment, Larry says, being a good tradesman is like having your own shop; you'll have people line up for you. They would say, "No, I want the Chinese guy to work on my boat. I don't want old Rick, I want Larry."

"And here's this guy," Larry adds, "he's in his early twenties and, y'know, I'm thirty at the time. And he just didn't want to be near me, because I was part Oriental."

Larry worked one summer at the Sunnyside Cannery. When fall came, BC Packers flew him back to Vancouver and put him to work through the winter at Celtic Shipyards, a repair shop on Celtic and Deering islands in the north arm of the Fraser River at the south end of Blenheim Street, just a few hundred metres upriver from the reserve. He was a mechanic for the fishing boats that headed out into the Salish Sea, when the salmon fleet was still one of the city's biggest employers.

When spring came, his foreman asked him if he would go up north again, this time to the BC Packers cannery at Namu, three hundred kilometres south of Prince Rupert. It was a good job offer; they wanted him to be in charge of the shop there. But when Larry asked his wife if she'd like to spend the summer in an isolated work camp on the Central Coast with a few hundred lonely men, she was not thrilled. He broke the bad news to his foreman, who told him, "That was the only reason we kept you on all winter. OK, see you. Pick up your cheque at 4:30, you'll be finished." Larry was out of work again.

This wasn't his last job with BC Packers though, or his last job in commercial fishing. About ten years later, Larry spent three months as second engineer on the *Quatsino*, a fish packer. More than two decades after that, in the late 1990s when he was thinking of retiring, he tried his hand at fishing himself at the urging of his brother Gordon, who had worked in the industry for close to fifty years, up and down the coast. Larry emulated him by buying a boat and spent a couple of summers on the Salish Sea, catching salmon. He loved being out on the open water, the feeling of freedom with the salt in his nostrils and the sun on his face. But he didn't like being alone at all hours far from land, and soon realized he was too old for it; the physical labour, hauling in nets and shovelling ice and packing fish, was just too intense for a diminutive man pushing sixty.

He could also see that the fish stocks, the huge runs of salmon, oolichan and herring that had nourished people up and down the BC coast for thousands of years, were in steady decline. "The overfishing was bad, and pollution," he says. "Now climate change is even worse. Just one degree of temperature rising in the water changes everything for the fish. It's closer to two degrees these days."

All these effects are less serious farther north, even though the Skeena canneries are all closed now. "The northern people are quite fortunate," Larry says. "Their runs are still there. They don't have the amount of pollution that we have in the Fraser. I have friends who go back up to Haisla territory and do the rendering of the oolichan to get the oil still."

Larry laughs at how ignorant people in BC have always been about Indigenous people. One time his aunt Mary applied for a job at the Gulf of Georgia Cannery, in Steveston, Richmond. The employment officer asked her nationality and she replied, "Indian."

"Well, we're not hiring Indians," they replied, thinking she was from India.

So she went back the next day, gave her name again, but answered "Hawaiian" this time. "OK, start work tomorrow," she was told.

"I thought it was OK to be Chinese at Steveston?"

"Yeah, but if you were Chinese, you would go through the Chinese labour broker," Larry explains, "the same as the East Indians do with the picking of the berries and things right now.

It's really sad how things were. People wouldn't get hired because they were of the wrong race or the wrong colour. It was quite prevalent."

//////////////

"They built fences all the way around the harbour," says Larry. He's standing on a grassy knoll at CRAB Park on the edge of Vancouver's Gastown, looking east towards the six huge orange cranes of the Centerm terminal jutting into Burrard Inlet, where container ships are being loaded. Chain-link fences topped with razor wire separate us from the huge stacks of brightly coloured containers in the terminal, labelled Hapag-Lloyd, Maersk, COSCO, China Shipping. "Can't get in without a swipe pass. It's been like this since 9/11; it's a strategic area, the port."

The whirr of a helicopter drowns out the conversation, landing at the floating Helijet pad to our left, carrying commuters from Victoria. A blue-and-white SeaBus taking passengers to North Vancouver slides smoothly out of the ferry terminal next door, past the bulk of *Grand Princess*, one of two massive cruise ships docked by Canada Place. A tugboat swings into view, pulling an old barge loaded with garbage, weaving between empty container ships riding high in the Inner Harbour, waiting to dock. A loon surfaces just below us, swallowing a fish, while Canada geese peck at algae at the waterline on the rocky beach. The helicopter's whirr is over-ridden by the screech of an old, black-and-red Canadian National locomotive on the tracks behind us, hauling a freight train weighed down with double-stacked containers. Float planes landing and taking off complete the panorama, the backdrop the jagged North Shore mountains, still capped with snow in May.

Vancouver is the largest port in Canada and the fourth-largest in North America by tonnes of cargo, thanks to a spectacular deep-water port, Burrard Inlet, just north of where Larry is standing; two smaller ports, on the main and north arms of the Fraser River; and its location as the western terminus of the trans-Canada railway and the continent's closest major port to Asia. For more than a century, the wheat from the vast farms of Canada's prairies has been loaded onto trains and brought to the shores of Burrard Inlet to be stored in huge concrete bins, transferred onto cargo vessels and shipped around the world, notably to Asia; Canada is the world's fourth-largest exporter of wheat, and its top three destinations are China, Japan and Indonesia. Huge quantities of many other products also flow through Vancouver's three ports, many in containers loaded and unloaded at facilities like Centerm, including cars, lumber, sulphur and canola oil.

For three decades, from 1968 when he lost his job at Celtic Shipyards to the day he retired in 1999, Larry worked on Vancouver's docks as a longshoreman. He registered one evening with the International Longshore Workers Union (ILWU), which had recently amalgamated all the import-export shops along Vancouver harbour in need of maintenance mechanics. They offered him a job that Monday, as a casual; he kept getting called back, and nine months later was inducted into the ILWU and hired full-time.

"That was the beginning of my longshore journey," Larry says. "You're always classified a longshoreman. I was in the maintenance shop, which included looking after just about everything: heavy-duty machinery, millwrighting, all the trades you're required to do." At Vancouver Wharves in North Vancouver, Larry's first long-term posting, they did most maintenance on site, welding equipment and pumps and maintaining bulldozers, cranes, forklifts, backhoes, even locomotive engines.

"My very first job was in a dock down here in Gastown," Larry says, pointing to the industrial area behind a fence. "They also had a site by where Science World is now. Then I was posted at Vancouver Wharves, which starts at Lions Gate Bridge by Capilano Creek, then goes eastward." He gestures across the harbour to the docks near the northern foot of the spectacular suspension bridge, instantly visible across the bay because of their blue roofs next to neon-yellow piles of sulphur. To their left we can see a splash of the green forest of Stanley Park, where a white tour bus is puttering past the squat lighthouse at Brockton Point.

The first engine Larry worked on was a three-cylinder John Deere tractor. He thought, "Holy smokes, that's a big machine." But he soon changed his mind: "It turned out to be a toy!" Soon he was working on Caterpillar bulldozers, front-end loaders, forklifts that could lift two thousand pounds (the big ones today can lift ten times that). When he worked for Canadian Stevedoring, he helped maintain container cranes and container straddle carriers. The latter are "like giant lumber carriers that pick up containers and drive them around the site to drop them off. They're two containers high, to be able to double-stack them."

As with trucks, the mechanics of these monstrously huge gizmos are surprisingly similar. "That little John Deere tractor, if you could blow it up to D9 size, it's the same," Larry says. "You're looking at the same problems, the same noises. There are different ways of adjusting all the tracks but it's basically all the same."

Larry's training as a machinist was highly useful. "It gives you a different outlook on the way different lubricants or metals behave," he says. "The accuracy of fit comes into play, it really opens up your eyes to that."

Even iron and steel, he learned, have a lifespan. Engines are like humans—they have internal flaws. The question is, which part has gone wrong, and why? "You get to learn that when you're machining, how you do the welding, how that can distort different things," Larry says. "Being a machinist is like learning a different language. You have a different worldview; you get to understand the way things are made."

A mechanic doesn't understand precision the way a machinist does; for a machinist, one-thousandth of an inch is huge. Taking something apart and putting it back together is quite different from machining, from actually creating it yourself. "A bore will have distortion of, say, four- or five-thousands of an inch," Larry says. "Two strands of your hair, a thick doobie paper!" He rolls thumb and fingers together suggestively. "That difference matters. It was really advantageous for me to have those machinist skills."

In his first sixteen years as a longshoreman, Larry was rotated between various wharves: Vancouver Wharves in North Van, twice; Canadian Stevedoring, the CPR wharf; Empire Stevedore, which had a couple of docks around Heatley Avenue on the south shore. Then in 1985, when he was the most senior machinist on the waterfront, he was asked to go to Western Stevedoring's Lynnterm Terminals, at the northern foot of the Second Narrows Bridge in North Vancouver. Computers were just coming online and Larry had catalogued all the parts in the Vancouver Wharves parts rooms, so they asked him to do the same thing at Western Stevedoring. He ended up running their parts room with one other longshore person for the next fourteen years.

Larry had first been introduced to micro-technology on the docks when Vancouver Wharves installed a brand-new machine equipped with micro-amps, tiny sensors. "You have exposed electrical parts working where there is potash, a salt basically, all over the site," he says. "It comes from Saskatchewan and is highly corrosive. It's in your fertilizer, though if you use too much of it, it'll choke off your grass." As soon as there was any hint of moisture—and there's always moisture on the waterfront, especially in the rainforest they call Vancouver—the machine would short out and the mechanics had to rush down and blow it dry to get it running again.

By the time Larry retired, everything on the docks had been computerized for a few years; now it's all digital, notably the lifting equipment, which has reduced damages a lot. "Everything is so precise now," he says. "They'll haul a trailer with containers on it, and it'll stop just short of hitting the ship. Then they lift it up, put it onto the ship, which may be rising or falling with the tide, or rising or falling with the unloading or loading of cargo—that's all calculated, they know it all, it's all programmed. Each ship is different, with its unique height in the water, it's all IT-driven now."

////////////

When Larry started working there, in the years after World War II, the docks were a tough, masculine world, with no time for polite language or how-do-you-dos. A lot of the men—and back then, it was pretty much all men—had fought in the war, sometimes on different sides, and they didn't hide their animosity towards men of other nationalities and ethnicities.

At the time, Larry was still using his dad's surname: Hong. So everyone considered him Chinese, though he rarely spoke about his ancestry, and certainly didn't mention his Musqueam side. Six months after meeting him, one guy he'd been working with came into the parts room and said, "Goddam it, Larry, you're not a Chinaman, you're an Indian!"

He replied, "Who told you I was a Chinaman?"

"Well, you got a Chinese name. We've been talking about this other Indian guy, who gets drunk and starts fights, you never said a word in his defence. You're not like that, you're here seven days, working late. Why the hell didn't you tell me?"

"First, I wanted to find out what you thought about Indians. I wanted to hear what you had to say about my mother. You were very derogatory."

"We're not talking about your mother!"

"Yes, you are—when you're putting Indian people down, saying they're lazy, you're talking about my mother."

"No, we're not!"

"Yes, you are! I know that you don't like Indians, and I don't know why you like me. I'm a real shit to you."

"That's the kind of language they use on the waterfront," Larry laughs. "And that was the kind of relationships we had, very straightforward. Most of the guys became friends; we had a job to do. People would say the same thing: you're here for the work, you're not here for the personal differences. We were taught in the machine shop, you can argue and fight, call each other different names, bad names, but come start time, you forget that, because you have a job to do, and you better do it right. The guys appreciated what I did, and we argued about things like the Indian Act and residential school."

Later, the guy in question apologized: "Sorry Larry, it's not about your mother." They developed an understanding and eventually grew to be good friends.

"That was part of the waterfront years, working with immigrants," says Larry. A lot of the men were from Yugoslavia or other parts of Soviet Eastern Europe who had married into different groups and had to make peace across families, with new in-laws who didn't like them because of their ethnicity or religion. "We'd be having coffee, having heated discussions in the parts room," says Larry. "The guys couldn't figure me out, I never get angry. I'm too physically small, I use the words I have to do my fighting. That's just as effective, sometimes more effective."

Larry thinks he learned the skill of strategic silence from his dad. He got that teenage job driving a three-ton truck by helping his father labouring. After a few days the boss had said to his dad, "He's a hard worker, that kid."

"What kid?" his dad replied.

"That one."

"Oh yeah, that's my son."

"How come you never told us before?"

"Well, you say what you got to say about my son. If it wasn't good, I wasn't going to tell you. But you're happy with his work, that's good."

For much of his life, keeping quiet and listening was a means for Larry to get information he wouldn't be afforded if people knew his complete background right away.

//////////////

The memory of the Mennonites' blackberry wine that he never did taste reminds Larry of his own struggles with smoking and drinking during his shop years. He started smoking much earlier, when he turned eleven. He had asked his parents for a cigarette a year or two earlier, and they'd told him he could smoke when he could afford to buy his own. When he started working alongside his mother on the farm, getting full pay as a labourer, he bought his first tin of tobacco and was soon rolling them up all the time. "I could roll cigarettes anywhere," he says with a laugh, gesturing to show off his one-hand technique. "I stopped in 1972 when I got some respiratory sickness, not sure if I got pneumonia or not but I couldn't smoke. I stopped once, twice, the third time was for good. Took me three years to quit."

After his first marriage ended in 1969, Larry spent a lot of time in bars after work, drinking beer with friends from the docks. He didn't think much about it until he bumped into a really good female friend who said, "I knew you drank, but I didn't know you were an alcoholic."

He protested at the time—"We met in a bar, you knew I drank!"—but her comment triggered something. That was 1982; he stopped drinking cold turkey and hasn't drunk since. Well, very rarely: "About a bottle of wine, plus a couple of beers, in forty-odd years," he says.

Larry found it harder to quit smoking than drinking. "Alcohol is not a physical addiction, it's an emotional addiction," he says. "I came to that realization after I'd stopped drinking for three months. I picked up a beer and waited for the urge to have another—and it didn't come. Six months later, same thing; twelve months, same. My mind said, it's not a physical addiction, it's emotional. Cigarettes, one puff is all it takes to be back to a couple of packs a day."

When he stopped drinking, he was surprised to discover he had to find a whole new cohort of friends, except for the ones who were *really* his friends. He used to go on regular fishing trips with several guys, but the spring after he quit drinking, they told him he wasn't invited anymore. "Our trips were expensive because of the booze we drank, and they said no, we don't want you. You know we're going to drink, and our wives will be mad at us if we're the ones who get you back on the booze."

///////////////

Looking back on all those years working on the docks, Larry says, "All my life I've done two jobs: fixing cars on weekends, fixing up the house. I'm physically conditioned for it." As a heavy-duty mechanic, he felt like he was doing calisthenics all day, up and down, under motors, back and forth in the shop. If he stopped at the end of the day, he'd fall asleep, so he never did. And he never injured his hands, thank God; "other people I know have lost fingers, lost the use of a hand."

The only thing he misses from the longshore work is the freedom. "We had a casual hiring system. If I felt like taking some time off, I'd talk to the foreman: I want two weeks off or whatever, call me a replacement." And they did, no questions asked. You did your shift, and when it was over, you were free. Now when he has to do a territorial acknowledgment or teach a class, the time is set in advance, there's no flexibility.

Thinking about it, Larry adds that he also misses the camaraderie. "My work life was always with men, women were a distraction," he says. When the first women welders turned up, the male dock workers were paralyzed. "All of a sudden there was a woman in the midst of all the swearing, the name-calling. How are we supposed to act around them? Do we have to say please and thank-you? Can't say a-hole or son-of-a-bitch. And you drank together, argued together. Discussed politics, religion. Couldn't do that with women around! Though I think they do now, because women are more common now, in the yard."

When he worked at Lynnterm Terminals, women from the office would sometimes come over, bringing documents for the foremen, and would tell the supervisor, it's like those guys are always fighting, they're yelling and swearing. "When that feedback came back, we said, 'We're in a shop, there's no time for politeness. Get your butt over here!'" Larry says with a laugh.

"We worked together, made good friendships, argued a lot, discussed our differences very openly, literally got in fights," he says more seriously. "But when you got to work, you worked together, it was part of the bonding. It was really a different way of working. My mentors [at school and M&M] were very civil, but once I got onto the waterfront, gutter talk was acceptable: the racial stuff, the different epithets, the swearing. Very politically incorrect language."

In July 2023, a quarter century after his last day on the docks, the ILWU asked Larry to come down and address a gathering during a big strike on the waterfront. His old shop had just received two citations for racist comments, both for slurs against South Asian workers. That turned out to be a sign of progress; he was pleasantly surprised at the faces looking out at him as he stood on the stage, a real mosaic of ethnicities from around the world, many of them women. As he spoke to the assembled workers about the importance of standing up for their rights, it felt like the British old-boys network that created the longshore union a century earlier had finally been broken.

To top it off, the five-week strike ended with an agreement the union embraced, including increased wages, benefits and training for dock workers. Larry had only played a small part, but he cheered the news.

"As longshoremen, we fought like stink to get a pension," Larry adds. He and some colleagues pressured the union to put a small amount, like ten cents for every hour worked, into a pension plan for all dock workers. But most of them didn't see the point, they wanted the money now. "And then they'd spend it, and when they were sixty-five they didn't have a penny!

"I could retire early because I am Indigenous and live on the reserve. Lots of other people couldn't."

So he did. In 1999, aged sixty-two. And began a whole new career.

Chapter Seven

Come On Home, Brother /
Back on Musqueam Reserve No. 2

"We're a civilization of grass farmers," Larry says. "We grow the grass to cut it and throw it away."

His gentle voice sounds like a shout over the swoosh and ping of golfers practising their swings at the driving range. We're in the parking lot of University Golf Course, looking at the green expanse dotted with signs marking 25, 50, 75 and 100 metres. In the background tall nets and trees tower over a manicured landscape dotted with flags and golfers in long shorts puttering about in white carts.

"The English would say this is not a waste of land, even though it's not producing anything, not even hay. Just producing little green carpets."

Larry's life story, like the story of the Musqueam people, has been shaped by a series of court cases—and both stories have been intertwined with the history of golf in Vancouver.

The beautiful green space we're looking at here, a relatively affordable public golf course next to the University of British Columbia, now belongs to the band, after they were awarded ownership of it and a neighbouring block of land as a result of talks ordered by the BC Court of Appeal in a 2007 court ruling. The band also received $20.3 million in cash and ownership of the Bridgeport Casino lands in Richmond, including the River Rock Casino.

The golf course negotiations had outraged many residents in the affluent Point Grey neighbourhood where it's located, the home riding of then-BC Premier Gordon Campbell, terrified their god-given right to cheap afternoons on the links was under threat. The dispute began when the Musqueam discovered that the province had sold the course, which sits on their traditional lands near the reserve, to the university for $11 million in 2003, without consulting them. The band challenged the legitimacy of the sale in court—asking the province, show us the document that says you own this land—and won. In the negotiations that followed, the Musqueam eventually promised they'd keep the land as a golf course until 2083, far longer than expected.

"We've come a long way to accommodate everybody, the golfers and everybody," said elected chief Ernie Campbell in the press conference after the deal was announced. Pushed on the protests from golfers, he famously added, "I wish that's the only problem I had for my people, where to golf. The majority of my community couldn't even afford green fees there, or the clubs."

For Larry, the irony is that "the rate payers out here say, 'Why are we giving it to the Indians, they are just going to develop it?' And it is already developed! The trees have been cut down, the land has been reshaped. And they are worried we are going to develop it and make some income off of it!" The "rate payers" have already clear-cut all of Metro Vancouver and developed it at a dizzying pace, a pace that is only increasing in the 2020s.

Never mind the irony that a lot of the original logging was done a century earlier by Musqueam fellers, including Larry's grandfather and several uncles and great-uncles.

The band were invited out to a town hall meeting during the negotiations. Larry thought it was crazy to go. But the chief's sister agreed to attend, and was shocked. "They wouldn't even let me talk!" she said afterwards. "As soon as I opened my mouth, everybody started yelling. They didn't want to hear a thing from Musqueam!"

The Great UBC Golf Course Battle was just one of many legal cases fought and won by the Musqueam that have helped shape Indigenous-government relations in Canada—and changed the path of Larry's life, by helping him and the band regain the rights they had long been denied.

The first key case, the Guerin case, was also about golf. It began in 1957, when the Indian Agent for the band leased 162 acres of Musqueam Reserve No. 2—more than 40 percent of the band's tiny pocket of land, one of the most densely populated in Canada—to the Shaughnessy Golf and Country Club on a seventy-five-year lease for a fraction of its value. The band only learned the terms thirteen years later when Chief Delbert Guerin gained access to Department of Indian Affairs archives. When he saw the contract, which was nothing like what the band had been told at the time, they decided to sue the federal government for not acting in their best interests.

Musqueam won the case and a $10-million settlement in 1979. This was overturned on appeal, so they took it to the Supreme Court of Canada. On November 1, 1984, the highest court in the land ruled in favour of the band. *Guerin v. The Queen* is considered a landmark case, establishing the precedent that Aboriginal rights impose an enforceable, pre-existing "fiduciary" responsibility upon the Crown. In other words, the government must act in the best interest of an Indian band in relation to its reserve lands.

In the wake of the 1984 ruling, the golf club lost another court case brought by the Musqueam, forcing it to pay its property taxes—now about $800,000 a year—to the band instead of the city. They've been doing that for forty-one years.

None of this has stopped the well-heeled patrons of the Shaughnessy Golf and Country Club from playing their rounds, driving their balls and carts around the lush green course and laughing when errant balls fly into reserve land or the Fraser River to the south, wining and dining in the clubhouse patios and Garden Lounge, all while the Musqueam, some of the poorest people in British Columbia, look on across the barbed-wire fences and badly pruned hedges that separate their crammed reserve from the links it surrounds. The course, called "a national treasure" by *Golf Business* and recently ranked the fifteenth-best in Canada, has hosted the Canadian Open four times. You can almost imagine Marie Antoinette in plaid plus-fours eating cake on the eighteenth green.

The course's seventy-five-year lease is set to expire in 2032, only seven years from now. What will the prestigious club do then, just walk away?

"Who knows? Who cares?" says Larry, smiling just a little. "They lied to us; they bullshitted us. They didn't care that was the wrong thing to have done. They never improved the payment of the lease, kept it at that low level for decades."

Within the next decade, the vast green expanse, once the site of a Big House and the grand stump from which Larry's grandfather distributed blankets at his potlatch, may well echo again to the sound of Musqueam singing and drumming. Maybe Larry's grandchildren will host a potlatch here, to celebrate their ties to Seymour Grant and all his ancestors who have lived at the mouth of the Fraser River since time immemorial.

/////////////

Most likely, the golf course land will echo to the sounds of Musqueam home-building; the band suffers from a critical shortage of housing, with a waiting list hundreds of members long. Larry himself has built two homes on the reserve in his lifetime. The first was in 1956–57, when he was still apprenticing, a gift for his mother to thank her for taking care of him. "A 'cabin' would be a more appropriate term to use," he says. "Twenty-four by twenty-four foot. It didn't have any indoor plumbing or water or lights. There was no access to water then." It was on land left by his grandfather Seymour, who died intestate.

(Larry chuckles at the ease with which this word rolls off his tongue. "It means 'without a will.' You wonder why I know all these legal terms? 'Fiduciary'? Half a life spent in court, proving I exist.")

Larry got all the materials to build his mum's cabin from Hudson Lumber, on Hudson Street in Marpole, just off Marine Drive. He couldn't pay up-front, but his uncle Tony went with him and proposed an installment plan. He had enough money for the cinder blocks and the beams, and the manager let him take the joists as well, as long as he promised to pay for them from his next two paycheques. They shook hands on the deal, which was renewed when he needed lumber to finish the job.

"That [white] man, whose family grew up in Marpole, had faith in the Aboriginal people at the time and could say, 'Here's a load of lumber worth forty dollars,' which was a lot of money, 'and this young boy here is going to come back two weeks from now and give you the [remaining] twenty dollars.' I believe it was Uncle Tony standing beside me that allowed that person to believe in me. I owe those two people a huge debt of gratitude."

Larry's gratitude for the second house he built on the reserve—this one much bigger, two storeys, with electricity, water, the works—goes to his younger brother Howard. The three brothers had been fighting to get their Indian status back since 1951, the year the federal restrictions on Indigenous people hiring lawyers were lifted, when Larry was just fifteen. But for many years it had seemed like an impossible battle. They couldn't find a lawyer who would take on Indigenous clients, and they didn't have the money to pay for one anyway. After spending five thousand dollars, the elder siblings were ready to drop it.

"All that time the community accepted us as band members, but we never got any land," Larry explains. "To get that, we'd have to go to court with our aunties, and we didn't want to do that. Didn't want to split the family, so we never contested that in court."

But Howard never gave up on the main fight. He continued preparing files and arguments, while Larry and Gordie, the ones with the best jobs, paid most of the legal bills. Larry doesn't know all the ins and outs, but the youngest Grant sibling finally found a willing advocate—times were changing—and relaunched the appeal in the early 1980s.

Just before their final day in court, early in April 1985, Howard called a family meeting to deliver some momentous news: federal Bill C-31 was set to pass, reinstating the status of Indigenous women who had lost it when they married non-Indigenous men. Maybe there was no point in continuing; Agnes was going to be vindicated, and they were going to get their status back anyway.

Larry disagreed. He had always been taught, "If you start a job, make sure you finish it. This had been in my mind for several decades. So I said, 'Let's go to court and let the chips fall where they may. Win or lose, let's finish it.' And lo and behold, the decision came down in our favour."

Thirty-four years after they'd begun the case, and forty-five years after the Indian agent had struck them off the Musqueam band roll and labelled them "the bastard children of Agnes Grant," the court accepted their appeal. Gordon, Larry and Howard got all their rights as Indigenous people back, retroactively to birth.

"I was born under the Indian Act, to a Status person, and it was the colonial law that took it away. And then gave it back, with all rights and privileges and inheritances." They didn't receive any money—they couldn't bear the idea of going back to court demanding damages—but the Grants and their children were now officially Musqueam again.

Larry was living in North Vancouver at the time. Howard, the only sibling who had never left the reserve, said, "Come on home, brother."

"It was a big thing," Larry says. "I'd been living off-reserve for more than twenty years," in a little house in a suburb, commuting to work, keeping his head down, trying to blend in. It was time to assume his Indigenous identity again. So he applied for a lot in a new subdivision on the reserve, and was granted an allocation of land. "So I came home to the reserve in the summer of 1985, and I've been in this house ever since. Built it from scratch, with my own funds."

Moving back to the reserve involved a total worldview shift. He'd gotten used to the Canadian way: be who you want to be, do what you want to, no need to get involved or know your neighbour. It was a shock to suddenly be surrounded by all these people who knew him and his family. "It was a big deal, to be recognized as a Musqueam band member again, in the land of your parents, grandparents, great-grandparents . . . to be part of the social community again." That means trying to help each other however you can; "often it's just being there, other times it's financial assistance, or food. To make sure things are OK."

All four Grant siblings now live on the reserve, with many of their children and grandchildren. Larry sat on the Musqueam Council for many years. His daughter Allyson Fraser has been on Council since 2001. Howard has sat on the Musqueam Council for even longer and was band manager for a while. Now he is executive director of the First Nations Summit, and his son Gordon is on the Musqueam Council. In April 2025, another of Howard's sons, Wade, was elected member of parliament for Vancouver Quadra in the federal election, off to Ottawa as part of Mark Carney's Liberal minority government.

vvvvvvvvvv

By the time Larry returned to the reserve in 1985, the Chinese farmers were long gone. Most of them had left en masse in the mid-1950s when the Department of Indian Affairs reduced all the agricultural leases to thirty days instead of yearly. "They couldn't operate with that short a notice," says Larry, "so they moved out."

The area where the farms once were had all been subdivided by then and is unrecognizable today, with new curving roads lined with suburban bungalows. A vacant lot lush with fireweed and lined with bright blue fencing marks the spot where the cook-shack once stood.

At the same time Larry was moving home, a Musqueam fisherman, Ronald "Bud" Sparrow, was beginning a six-year battle over his right to catch salmon in the waters bordering the reserve. Like the Guerin case, *Regina v. Sparrow* (1990) would go all the way to the Supreme Court of Canada—who once again would rule in favour of Musqueam, in another national precedent.

The band has fished in the Fraser for millennia. When Europeans began settling on the river's banks in the 1800s, it was thick with salmon, with huge runs of returning fish turning the water red and green every fall. This is not an exaggeration— expert estimates put pre-contact numbers in the many tens of millions, with at least eight million sockeye, the most highly valued of the six species, passing through Musqueam lands on their epic migration upriver every year.

It must have been a phenomenal spectacle, the glittering armies of dying fish, missiles of pure muscle, massing at the mouth of the river for the mighty assault on the cataracts and pools ahead of them. And all the way up the river for hundreds of kilometres, men with nets, traps and harpoons catching the silver-flashing fish as they cruised through eddies and leapt up roaring rapids, while the women dried the carcasses on wooden racks and smoked the succulent orange meat for the lean months ahead. If British Columbia has some of the most sophisticated Indigenous cultures on earth, it's because of the salmon. And the

Musqueam are the first Salmon People, the people of the mouth of staləẃ, the mighty Fraser River.

The first commercial cannery was established in the late 1800s at Celtic Slough by Deering Island, just a few hundred metres upriver from the Musqueam reserve; Larry worked there in the winter of 1967–68. It and the dozens of others that soon followed employed Europeans, First Nations, Chinese and Japanese workers, but most of the fishermen feeding the industrial packing process were Musqueam, later joined by many Japanese, who also faced severe racism. By 1902, even the owner of Celtic, as quoted in the 2007 book *The Story of Dunbar*, was complaining about overfishing, saying "the fishing grounds extend for only about 25 miles up the River's mouth and in this distance 48 canning operations are in operation. The industry is in a deplorable condition."

The "salmon rush" was followed by the first forced closures as fish numbers began to drop a century ago. A complete fishing ban on the Fraser was enforced from 1919 to 1923 after a rock slide in the Fraser Canyon blocked the annual migration. Commercial fishing still continues, but it never really recovered from this collapse. Overfishing, pollution and now climate change have decimated a resource the Musqueam and all the coastal nations once relied on as a staple food supply; wild herring and salmon are down to less than a tenth of their once-spectacular abundance.

Enter Bud Sparrow. One May day in 1984, he was arrested while fishing for chinook salmon with a drift net nearly twice the legal length allowed by his "food-fishing" licence. The Musqueam decided to fight the charge, arguing that band members had a right to fish on their ancestral land. They highlighted Section 35 of Canada's new constitution, signed into law two years earlier by Queen Elizabeth II and Prime Minister Pierre Elliott Trudeau, which "affirms" all "existing Aboriginal and treaty rights of the Aboriginal peoples of Canada." The Musqueam argued this included fishing on the Fraser River, which they'd been doing since long before there was a Queen or a Prime Minister Trudeau, I or II, let alone a Canada, a Supreme Court or a constitution.

After three defeats in British Columbia, the Musqueam took the case all the way to the Supreme Court of Canada in 1988. Two years later, Sparrow won. The court agreed that the Musqueam's right to fish had not been extinguished and couldn't be limited without clear justification—which did not include overfishing by non-Musqueam people. For the first time in Canada's history, a court had acknowledged that Indigenous people had rights that predate the country's existence.

"Musqueam proved that we had done that fishing and we were allowed to have a commercial section of it," says Larry. "That is the Sparrow case, and that one stood above the Guerin case and went around the world also."

When they were fighting the Guerin and Sparrow cases, which took five and six years respectively, the band were constantly worried about going bankrupt. Larry remembers talking to Chief Delbert Guerin then and being told, "If we go to court, we'll have to tighten up our belts for a minimum of ten years. We'll be broke. We won't have any money in our bank."

"And the old folks said, 'Go. Do what is right. If it costs us, it costs us,'" he says. "And they won both times." Only now is the band being compensated, slowly, for sacrifices made over generations. They have their limited commercial fishery, and the Shaughnessy Golf and Country Club taxes, and are getting ready for more opportunities to come.

"These resources—the fish, the land—belong to the community," says Larry. "We want what is right, what is ours rightfully."

Even the Government of Canada is realizing that salmon and other precious resources are finite and worth protecting. In 2023, for instance, the feds undertook a six-week project to create a breach in the North Arm Jetty, just west of the Musqueam reserve, to restore natural migration pathways for juvenile salmon and other fish species and recreate the natural movement of freshwater and fine sediments in the Fraser estuary. More than a century after it was built, the jetty is no longer blocking salmon from going up the river, returning to their birth pools as they've done for millennia.

///////////////

So, does Larry golf? Well, Howard once convinced him to buy a set of clubs, but he never got the hang of it and soon gave them to Howard. Years later, his stepdaughter was invited to go golfing with a group of women, so Howard lent her the clubs.

"I can play, but I'm not sure why they invited me. What do I do?" she asked Larry.

"Just keep your head down and listen," Larry told her.

When she came back from her day on the links, she was in shock. "These ladies are no good at golf! They can barely hit the ball. All they do is talk and talk and talk, about other women and business."

"So, was it fun?"

"Totally. And they gave me all sorts of names of people to contact. They know everyone. It's not a sport, it's networking!"

That's what grass farming produces: networks.

Chapter Eight

The City Before the City /
At c̓əsnaʔəm, in Marpole

Close to forty years ago, Larry visited New York City for the first time. He was doing research, travelling with a group called the Musqueam Weavers, who were studying traditional textiles. On US Thanksgiving, they were invited to a loft in Greenwich Village, still the bohemian heart of Manhattan back then, by a Musqueam Elder and a professor who was studying shamanism.

An earnest white woman who worked in the Library of Congress caught Larry alone for a moment. "You're so fortunate," she said. "You have all this history."

"You should look at it from my side," Larry replied. "I'm an Indian, and I'm part Chinese."

"I'm not talking about that," she replied. "We've been here four hundred years, my family came from Germany. But I don't know where they came from, who they were. And we've moved around all the time. You know your family, community and culture; I do not. I have no idea where I come from." That's what Larry means when he talks about the "refugee immigrant settler mindset"—a displaced people who come and go, chasing jobs and riches across the continent, ravaging the resources and the land and then moving on.

He knows exactly where he comes from: an ancient village called c̓əsnaʔəm. Centuries before they were penned in on Musqueam Reserve No. 2, his ancestors lived and traded here. A National Historic Site since 1933, it now sits at the foot of Montcalm Street and Southwest Marine Drive, in the shadow of the Arthur Laing Bridge, under a filthy flyover in a light industrial zone thousands of Vancouverites drive past every day on their way to and from the suburbs or the airport.

In 400 BCE, c̓əsnaʔəm was one of the largest settlements in what is now British Columbia, on the north bank of the Fraser River near its then mouth, seven kilometres upstream from its mouth today. It is one of the largest middens in Canada, more than twenty-five hundred years of shellfish debris and human belongings spread over two hectares. Much of the site was destroyed when the Fraser Arms Hotel was built over it in the 1950s; the rest was threatened in 2011, when the Musqueam discovered that the province had issued a permit for the construction of a residential building right on top of the midden. The struggle that followed brought the band together in an epic communal protest that lasted more than two hundred days and put their deep roots in Vancouver into the national spotlight for the first time.

///////////////

"You know what a midden is, Larry?" asked British Columbia Premier Christy Clark. "It's a garbage pile, that's all it is." Larry met the province's leader at Norma Rose Elementary School, near UBC, in the middle of the protest. "Everyone else was saying, a midden is a history book, all the different belongings and things that were forgotten or discarded there are signposts of civilization," he says. "But to her, it was just a garbage pile."

Larry says this in the parking lot in front of Value On Liquor Store—"Below Government Prices, Open Everyday 9 am–11 pm."—by the entry ramp to the Arthur Laing Bridge, which leads to Vancouver International Airport or YVR. The whole scuzzy complex—the liquor store, Dollarama, Thai Son restaurant, Kar Store used vehicles next door—used to centre on the Fraser Arms Pub. "It was a handy place for air hostesses and pilots to stay," explains Larry. "It was the closest one to YVR, just across the bridge." In his younger days he remembers having a drink at the bar here once or twice.

It barely merits a sideways glance from motorists passing by now, but the little mall sits right on top of one of the most important archaeological sites in Canada. Early excavators called it Eburne, the Great Fraser Midden, or the Marpole Midden. The Musqueam, who now own it, have always called it c̓əsnaʔəm, the largest settlement of their people pre-contact. A film and exhibition about the fight to save it produced by the Museum of Vancouver called it "the city before the city."

People have been digging up bones and artefacts here for close to a hundred and fifty years, ever since workers building a road through the rich alluvial soil on a bend in the Fraser River started pulling treasures out of the earth in 1883. An excavation by the American Museum of Natural History sent many artefacts, plus about seventy-five human bodies, to New York. British-born archaeologist Charles Hill-Tout conducted a more thorough dig in the 1920s and '30s and sent more artefacts abroad, mostly to museums in Europe frantically filling out their Northwest Coast collections during the waning days of empire. He estimated the midden covered at least two hectares and was from two to five metres deep, making it one of the largest in North America, challenged in size only by the massive middens on Denmark's coast, also thousands of years old. Among the countless clam and mussel shells, Hill-Tout found all sorts of refined artefacts: antler carvings shaped into birds' heads, dog-tooth necklaces, whale-bone bracelets, antler and bone harpoons and daggers, wooden adzes with nephrite blades. His self-taught assistant, Herman Leisk, extracted many of these for the precursor of the Museum of Vancouver, including the skeletons of more than seven hundred and fifty people, most of which he then disposed of because of space constraints.

"The railroad track goes through, it cuts into the site," says Larry. He's at the edge of the parking lot now, overlooking a steep embankment covered in blackberry bushes. A guy in a flannel shirt on his break is having a smoke to our left, enjoying the more scenic view across the Fraser River towards the airport. "There are still belongings in there. Pot hunters used to come and take them. That's all part of the midden too, where the bus depot is," Larry adds, pointing towards a vast transit centre by the river where several hundred of the city's electric buses are parked.

"Pot hunters have been coming here since day one, because it's a huge, rich site. It goes all the way up to about 70th Avenue, and as far as Hudson Street, way behind. That's all part of the settlement." It covers close to eight city blocks, much buried beneath an ugly netherland of on-ramps and four-lane roadways. This is the respect Canada pays to its National Historic Sites.

~~~~~~~~~~

c̓əsnaʔəm hit the headlines in January 2012 when the Musqueam learned that human remains had been found by a developer digging the foundations of a five-storey, 108-unit apartment complex.

Word spread quickly on the reserve, and soon Musqueam protestors were blocking the site. Construction was suspended for four weeks; the developer then applied for permission to remove the remains and carry on.

In response, more than a hundred band members and supporters marched to c̓əsnaʔəm. In no time they were holding vigils around the clock, drumming and singing and making themselves seen and heard. During the day they handed out pamphlets to confused motorists. At night, they sat around the campfire telling stories.

"We come from a sacred place called c̓əsnaʔəm," Aaron Wilson, a lawyer and band member, says in the film. "It's a village, a hub, a named place. More importantly, it's a connection, to our history, our ancestors, who we are as a people. More than any one of those things, it's invested with many different meanings."

Larry was at the protest from the beginning, though he didn't approve of the singing and drumming; he was worried they would disturb the ancestors buried there. He remembers talking to bus drivers, who would stop and say, "What the hell are you doing, get out of our way!" as they drove out of the depot.

"We would give them pamphlets and tell them," he says. "They got it right away, after that they'd be honking," he says, making a waving gesture. "And that happened on the bridge too, we gave pamphlets to the drivers who were swearing at us for creating a traffic jam. We told them the issue, they said 'OK, that's fine.'"

"So you were there when they blocked the bridge?" This was a step-up in the protest after several months of stalemate, shutting down access to the airport for two hours and getting the issue on the news for the first time.

"We didn't block the bridge, we just walked over," says Larry with a smile. "There may have been a couple of hundred of us, but we were just walking over."

"Had to get to the other side of the river?"

"Yeah. Giving our message. For me, that's what we were doing. We just walked over. Took a whole traffic lane. It was a march, to express our views and show the importance of this area. That caught their attention very quickly, and disrupted YVR."

To the Musqueam's surprise, the reaction was mostly positive. Many people interviewed agreed with their outrage; some even asked why they hadn't protested earlier. To which Larry says, "If we'd done this two or three decades earlier, we would have been marched out of here by the RCMP with guns."

"The neighbourhood people came, brought food," he adds. "One of the businesses brought something for us to eat every day, enough for five or ten people. We had a lot of local support, from different communities: Native communities and others too, like unions.

"There were Musqueam banners put up here," he says, pointing to a fence now covered with a printed ċəsnaʔəm poster. "They became our backdrop."

Both Aaron and Larry noted how the language slowly changed as the protest developed and sympathy for the Musqueam grew. At the start, the media talked about a "midden" or "refuse pile" and said "the Musqueam claim it's a historic site." Six months later, they were calling it a village, not a garbage heap, and a National Historic Site, with no qualifications.

For Larry, the biggest shift was from talking about "objects" or "artefacts" to the more personal "belongings." "I call them *belongings*, because people are buried with things that are important to them," he says. "Or they are important to the family that is putting away their loved ones, for that person to be in the other world, the spiritual world, with their belongings with them . . . They belonged to somebody, they didn't just appear in some pile of dirt." We don't talk about the ruins of Troy or Tutankhamun's tomb as garbage dumps.

On September 27, 2012, the Musqueam learned that the province would not be renewing the permits for development. In their explanation, they cited c̓əsnaʔəm's status as a National Historic Site. In the negotiations that followed, the band bought back part of the site.

So what does c̓əsnaʔəm mean to Larry? "It means that this is a community our people lived on," he replies. "It's the evidence that we were here, that we're still here. The evidence shows it was a major trading port, this area. Our people were always in trade, up and down the coast and across the continent, thousands of years ago.

"The Aboriginal people in our communities were very sophisticated," he continues. "Still are. They created many things and did that with the accuracy of computerized equipment. And then our people were architects, on land, on the sea. They were sophisticated with medicines and spirituality. And lived culturally."

The Musqueam saved c̓əsnaʔəm, but the battle isn't over. The site still looks like an abandoned lot, next to a used-car dealership and a bus depot. "There was talk of putting up a kiosk here, hasn't happened yet," says Larry, peeking over the chain-link fence that protects it. "Some said, now we can put up a building! We were, 'No, we didn't want a building, that's why we fought for it!' We could have a little park and an info kiosk, so people understand what this is really about."

A park has been mocked up but no funds have been found yet. "That's the trick," says Larry. "It would be a good way to educate Vancouverites about their history."

///////////////

"Did the Aztec and Mayan civilizations that have astounded antiquarians and archaeologists since the Spanish conquest of Mexico, pass this way before taking root and maturing in the southern lands?" So begins a typical early newspaper article on the Marpole Midden, under the shocked headline, "Relics of Prehistoric Race Show Considerable Artistic Skill."

Larry shakes his head talking about these age-old conspiracy theories. He's sitting on a wooden bench in Marpole Park, a couple of blocks away from the midden. "Maybe the Aztecs and Mayans should have come up north, get away from the Spanish."

The Musqueam have a long way to go when it comes to educating Vancouverites about their history (the Vancouver Art Gallery, founded in 1931, has never had a historical gallery; like the whole city, it focuses on the contemporary). Ever since the midden was "discovered," the "experts" have been repeating the strange logic of that newspaper story, distancing the finds from the local Indigenous people because of their sophistication or elaborate theories around displacement and migration. The Bering Land Bridge model of how the Americas were populated assumes that during the last ice age, war-like Asian immigrants crossed into Alaska and headed south into the Americas, killing mammoths and massacring enemies as they went. This theory conveniently implies that when the European colonizers arrived, they were just another wave of violent settlers, like the mammoth-hunters before them. As one critic put it, "American Indians were not original inhabitants of the Western hemisphere but latecomers who had barely unpacked before Columbus came knocking on the door."

Like tales of human sacrifice and scalping, this theory, taught to generations of schoolchildren, doesn't just justify the ruthlessness of European settlement. It also questions Indigenous claims that they have been living in places like Vancouver since time immemorial. Hence the suggestion that it must have been Aztecs or Mayans who settled c̓əsnaʔəm. The only problem is, the scientific data to support this is murky at best; how do you explain carbon dating that shows continuous settlement up and down the BC coast for at least four thousand years, sometimes many more? Not to mention oral history, which talks of thousands of years of stable society.

The West Coast's oldest middens, footprints of ancient villages, correspond to places where fish and shellfish were once abundant. In the Vancouver area, the oldest ones are farther and farther up the Fraser, forty and even fifty kilometres from its current mouth, where the sea must have reached five or six thousand years ago as the delta formed after the ice age. The ones as far upriver as q̓íc̓əy̓ (Katzie, near Maple Ridge) predate c̓əsnaʔəm by several millennia. One of the oldest archaeological sites in BC is at Namu, site of the cannery Larry almost worked at on the Central Coast near Bella Bella; stone blades found there have been dated to 8250 BCE, more than ten thousand years ago.

When archaeologist Charles Hill-Tout unveiled a cairn to the Marpole Midden at Marpole Park in 1933, to celebrate its new status as a National Historic Site, he talked about the "birth of Vancouver" and called "these melancholy monuments" a link between primitive and modern times. Three hundred people came to the rollicking civic celebration, but no Musqueam were present, or invited. A *Vancouver Sun* editorial on the unveiling extolled, "A civilization is being built on the ruins of dumps and refuse heaps formed by natives in prehistoric times."

At this point Larry loves recounting the story of Kennewick Man, an ancient, complete skeleton found in a riverbank in Oregon near the border with Washington state in 1996. The archaeologists of the time reconstructed the man's skull and saw that it was long and thin. "Hah, he's European, let's carbon-date him and find a match," says Larry in his best curatorial voice. They sent the skeleton around the world, searching for DNA similarities. This went on for ten years, fruitless: no match. "We can't figure it out, where the hell did this guy come from?" Larry says with a chuckle.

Then the Colville tribe from Washington, in the Spokane area not far from where Kennewick Man was found, gave some DNA samples. "And by some miracle, there was a match! They couldn't believe it. This skeleton carbon dated to about 8,500 years ago, and the match was local. The tribe still exists. They're just below Penticton there, on the American side.

"So our people have been here for thousands of years! We're not from Central America, we're not from Mongolia."

"Here!" says Larry with a big smile, gazing out at the green foliage of Marpole Park and the towering monument to c̓əsnaʔəm / The Marpole Midden in the June sunshine.

"That's where I'm from. Here!"

Chapter Nine

On Campus /
At the University of British Columbia

"It's been a long time coming," says Larry. He's sitting on a concrete bench in the sunshine next to the Musqueam Post, which rises from a sumptuous plant and water feature running down University Boulevard towards East Mall in the centre of the University of British Columbia. Carved by Musqueam artist Brent Sparrow Jr. from a huge cedar log and installed with much ceremony in 2016, the pole is a larger-than-life standing human figure entwined in the coils of sʔiːɬqəy̓, the double-headed snake whose droppings gave birth to the məθkʷəy̓ plant.

It's a peaceful, meditative spot where Larry likes to sit when he's on campus (he's an adjunct professor but does most of his language teaching on the reserve; he comes here to mentor students at the First Nations Longhouse, and to give regular territorial acknowledgements and Musqueam welcomes). A good spot to think about the Musqueam's complicated relationship with British Columbia's oldest and most prestigious university, ranked the third-best in Canada, proud of the eight Nobel laureates, seventy-four Rhodes scholars and three Canadian prime ministers it has produced, including recent PM Justin Trudeau.

UBC was founded in 1908 with an act of the provincial government. No money was pledged; instead, a separate BC government act provided for the funding of the university through an endowment of land, later specified as 1,214 hectares of Point Grey, a forested peninsula ten kilometres west of downtown Vancouver. The land—which today includes UBC's vast main campus, 401 hectares or four square kilometres across; an area twice that size that became Pacific Spirit Regional Park in 1989; and many other smaller parcels—is all unceded Musqueam territory, right next to their main reserve (which is only 162 hectares, 13 percent of UBC's endowment). The Musqueam were barely consulted during these transactions, or later while the university was funding its growth by selling or developing the land; about 280 hectares have been subdivided and sold as residential, commercial and recreational property over the last century. The university finally signed a "memorandum of affiliation" with the band in 2006, ninety-eight years after its founding, and the two groups have worked together on various projects since, like installing hən̓q̓əmin̓əm̓ street signs in 2018, two years after the sʔiːɬqəy̓ post was raised.

"Reconciliation is a long-term process," Larry says diplomatically, looking up at the post and the plantings around it, which are designed to evoke the pre-contact marshland by the Fraser River. "It means a lot to us to have Musqueam recognition and acknowledgment on campus, in a very public space. Not hidden away some place, sitting behind some tree like the qiyəplenəxʷ (Capilano) Post at Allard Hall," another work by Sparrow installed in less enlightened times: 2012.

Before 1912, when it began to be logged, Point Grey was mostly dense rainforest, trimmed with rocky beaches to the west and marshland to the north. There were no Musqueam settlements in what is now UBC or Pacific Spirit Park, as far as we know, but there were permanent settlements all around the perimeter by the sea. There are also natural clearings and meadows in the forest where medicinal plants grew and deer grazed.

"Trails criss-crossed between the communities, from the river to the inlet," Larry says. "But there were never any stories that mentioned people living in what is now the campus. It was a place where we gathered our medicines, and some of our foods, the materials for food and houses and canoes. That's what it was used for."

Then, as now, this beautiful spot was a place apart, an area for meditation and education: "We used to use it for ceremonial and spiritual retreat, for rejuvenation. It's very much like being out in the ocean, just you and the ocean, you can come to terms with yourself; others can do the same in the forest. Go into the forest on their own, or many times together, and just kind of coming to peace, coming to terms, very much like we take off for a few weeks and go for a hike or just go camping somewhere and reflect on our life.

"It's all about the training, the discipline it takes to live within the forest by yourself, or just a couple of you. You have to learn all the discipline that comes with that. Part of the training is learning about all the vegetation that is safe to use and not safe to use. So it's been a place of learning, of physical and emotional learning, for a long time." A fitting location for a university.

/////////////

With high cliffs overlooking the mouth of Vancouver Harbour, the Strait of Georgia and Vancouver Island beyond, the campus is a very strategic spot. It was a military reserve during both world wars, and many of the university's first buildings were army barracks. The military connection goes much further back though. In 2011 the Musqueam gifted the name q̓ələχən to a new student residence building in Totem Park, after the fortified site where the famous chief qiyəplenəxʷ (anglicized as Capilano), Larry's great-great-grandfather, lived with the families of other warriors in the late 1700s.

qiyəplenəxʷ and his warriors welcomed the first English and Spanish invaders to the shores of what we now call Vancouver from the cliffs above Wreck Beach, beginning with Spanish navigator José María Narváez, the first European to enter Vancouver Harbour, in 1791, followed in 1792 by British captain George Vancouver, who gave it the name Burrard Inlet in honour of a former shipmate. As he sailed back through First Narrows, now spanned by the Lions Gate Bridge, Vancouver was surprised to see Spanish ships moored off what is now Jericho and Locarno beaches to the north of where we're standing—that's why he called the beaches "Spanish Banks."

"We speak very fondly of qiyəplenəxʷ," says Larry. "We call him our warrior-general, because he was the one who helped maintain our Aboriginal laws and culture, and a lot of our spirituality. And defended the river that is called Fraser today, against people who were coming to invade our territory." Larry's younger brother, Howard E. Grant, now bears the name qiyəplenəxʷ, after Larry gave it to him in a ceremony in the Big House.

qiyəplenəxʷ and his men were mostly Musqueam, and they fought many battles from their fort situated below what is now MOA (the Museum of Anthropology at UBC). "The lookouts were high up and the fortified site was down on the beach level,"

Larry says. "You could see from the point right across to Point Atkinson [by Lighthouse Park in West Vancouver]. The families had a signal system watching for strangers coming from up the Salish Sea or down the Puget Sound area. That way, you could see who was coming."

The cliffs were used in similar fashion during World War II, when the Canadian government was preparing for a Japanese invasion by sea. Two light stations were installed on the beach, in front of MOA and the university president's house next to it, with huge concrete gun emplacements above. One still stands on the south side of MOA, and another one inside the museum was turned into a plinth for the famous carving *The Raven and the First Men* by Haida artist Bill Reid.

Larry walks over to a map of the area mounted at the top of the cliff, pointing out all these sights. "Here, in front of the anthropology building, there's a little mound that's also a gun emplacement. And there was another gun emplacement in Stanley Park, and a lighthouse on the North Shore where the Capilano River enters. You can actually see the whole Strait of Georgia, the Salish Sea, from this vantage point."

həm̓ləsəm̓ is one of two UBC Totem Park residences gifted with Musqueam names in 2011. The second one is q̓ələχən, after a transformation site on Wreck Beach, at the foot of the cliff below the residence. Larry points out the locations on the map and explains the name.

"Our transformer at that time was named χe:l̓s. He was here to make things right. Everything was here already but some things, some people, were not right, and he was the transformer who came along and helped people. The ones that didn't respond to the encouragement to make things right socially were sometimes changed into animals or rocks. In the area we call q̓ələχən on Wreck Beach, there is a natural spring, and a greedy man decided that was going to be his private domain; 'This is mine.' People came by asking for water, but he wouldn't share. He'd just play with the water and waste it.

"After a while, a time of discussion, χe:ƚs decided to transform him into a rock, which he did. He also transformed a little container he had beside him into another rock. So there are a pair of rocks down in that beach area that represent that. They're still there alongside the shore.

"What that represented, when we named that second house həṁləsəṁ, was something that happens here and at other institutions—you have to share resources. That young man wouldn't share and was changed into a rock. Today at the universities, you have to share all your resources, and if you don't you might be transformed into a lump on a log"—he chuckles—"in the sense that you don't advance, you just become a lump.

"You come as a student to the university to learn things and transform yourself into the person you think you want to be in your life. However, many times you come in thinking you're going to be one thing, but because people share resources, like knowledge, your life gets transformed into something else, something that you never even thought of."

⁕⁕⁕⁕⁕⁕⁕⁕

"There was hunting here," Larry adds with a wide sweep of his hands to indicate the whole campus, where trees once ruled supreme. "There were elk, some deer, black bears." As a teenager he remembers one of the last times the Musqueam hunted here together, after someone spotted a couple of deer in the forested area now called Pacific Spirit Park. "A few people came along and got the deer, and we had a feast," he recalls. "Deer aren't seen there much anymore; every once in a while one swims over from Bowen Island or somewhere like that. The Department of Wildlife gets called in and they transport it back out."

There were also lots of small mammals, especially raccoons. All of them have decreased in number or disappeared altogether, especially since the half-dozen streams, all salmon-bearing, were covered up and run through culverts.

The forest was also a source of cedar, the most important forest resource in Musqueam culture. "That may look like a large cedar," Larry says, pointing to a towering tree beside Main Mall, "but it's not, compared to the trees that were here before. When we were kids there were stumps that were at least two and a half, three metres across, and at least three metres off the ground, throughout the Endowment Lands. That's how large the trees were."

Pacific Spirit Park and the many green spaces on UBC campus are all second-growth forest. The biggest trees are a little over a hundred years old and impressive, but they are saplings next to the massive fir and cedar that once stood tall in the primeval temperate rainforest that covered all of today's Vancouver when Larry's grandfather Seymour Grant was a boy, giants five and six hundred years old and thirty to forty metres tall. Walking through the park you see many huge stumps, a reminder that this lovely forest with its bike trails and little streams is a pale shadow of its former, majestic self.

Cedar had many uses, including roof beams, support posts and horizontal boards for longhouses. "The boards would over-lap, like this," explains Larry, putting one hand slightly over the other. Cedar bark is still used to make hats and other clothing, including capes, and for the baskets Larry's grandmother Mary Charlie once made. The inner bark is crushed and woven into fine textile material for clothing, capes and hats, and for building houses and canoes. "We also use it in spiritual ceremonies, and the cedar bark branches too," says Larry. "So that tree was multi-purpose, interdisciplinary. We need that in life."

The area that is now UBC campus was logged in 1912. Many of the loggers were Indigenous—including Larry's grandfather Seymour and several of his sons, Larry's uncles. "They helped to log out Point Grey!" Larry says with a mix of pride and sadness.

"They did it all with saws and axes," says Larry, making sawing and then chopping motions with his hands. "They got eight-foot or ten-foot bucksaws, cut those huge trees to ten feet off the ground. My grandfather never spoke of it, but my uncles did. They did logging all over BC."

Even today, feller and high rigger are high-risk jobs; that's why they call the big trees "widow-makers."

"The high rigger, he sets up the spar tree, the highest in the area," Larry says. "First he has to top it, using a girth you wrap around the trunk; then he uses it to haul the trees to the loading area. But when they top that tree, it could split."

Larry's uncles used to say chokerman was even more perilous. "He sends the sling around the log, then signals, and they highline it. That picks up the log, but it could pick up a whole bunch of other stuff. You got to be jumping out the way real fast!"

Still, logging's a lot better paid than picking berries or hops, now as then. His papa and uncles were willing to risk their lives to earn danger money, facing down the widow-makers of Point Grey.

Musqueam oral history says that the people knew about the orcas and porpoises that lived out in the Gulf, but as far as Larry understands, they didn't hunt them very often. The Musqueam did not see orcas as "killer whales" but rather as beneficial animals who sometimes helped human beings. "Orcas were called 'blackfish' by a lot of our Elders," he explains. "Blackfish were the ones that would save you when you were out on the sea; many times they'll come along and escort you. They weren't actually sacred, but you had extra respect for them." Not so seals and sea lions, which the men hunted from canoes for their meat, blubber and oil.

The Musqueam also harvested kelp along the beach; precontact, kelp was food, and as a young man Larry and his friends also gathered it, dried it and sold it to merchants in town, who used it to make food and medicine. "Either Chinese or the private drugstores that used to be around, long before London Drugs took over," he says.

"We also gathered herring eggs; there were herring that spawned around the point area," he says, pointing to an area near MOA. "Herring roe is a real delicacy, a very rich food, rich in oil, vitamins and nutrients."

The Musqueam also fished from the beach for smelt—eaten right away—and salmon and oolichan, which they dried on racks. The herring and oolichan are long gone from the mouth of the Fraser, but a few oolichan, which once thrived in huge numbers all the way to Hope, can still be caught around the Port Mann Bridge area. "They used to get mussels and clams around here too," Larry says, "and crabs—in my mother's generation, around 1900, 1910. After that there were none left."

Larry by the pond in leləm̓, November 2024.

Larry's maternal grandparents,
Seymour and Mary Charlie Grant, c. 1930.

A formal portrait of Larry's father, Hong Tim Hing, c. mid 1920s. He probably had it taken to send back to China to show he was doing well.

Agnes Grant (centre), Larry's mother, with her sister Edna (left) and a second cousin, sometime in the 1920s.

A formal portrait of Agnes and Tim Hing and family, minus Howard, taken at Yucho Cho studio in Chinatown in 1940. Baby Helen stands between her mum's legs, Larry his father's, while Gordon stands on the right.

The four Grant siblings in 1947. Larry on the right is standing on a box so Gordon doesn't tower over him; Helen holds Baby Howard.

Larry holding his baby brother Howard on the farm, c. 1950.

Larry (left) joking with a Musqueam worker at St. Mungo's fish cannery, on staɬəẃ in Delta, near where the Alex Fraser Bridge now stands.

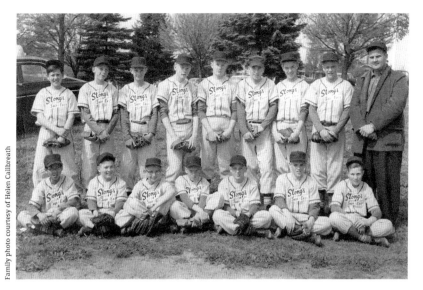

Howard, bottom row far left, was shortstop on a local baseball team, Dunbar Stong's—and the first Indigenous kid to play organized baseball in the area. Stong's still has a grocery store on Dunbar Street.

Larry between his mum, right, and Aunt Edna, dressed in her travelling clothes, off to Sardis to pick hops.

Larry in Agassiz, February 2023, near the field where he was born on a hot August night 86 years earlier.

Larry in Mission City, February 2023, by the foundations of the girl's dormitory of St. Mary's residential school.

The base of the Reconciliation Pole at UBC showing the bronze spindle whorl by Musqueam carver Kayám̓ Richard Campbell and Haida carver James Hart, who also carved the pole.

Scott Steedman

Scott Steedman

Larry accepting an honorary Doctor of Laws degree from Simon Fraser University in October 2023.

A house board on the reserve near Larry's house,
carved for Expo 86 by Stan Green.

Left to right and eldest to youngest, the three brothers in November 2023:
Gordon, Larry and Howard E. Grant.

Most of the 6.7 kilometres of Wreck Beach, Vancouver's westernmost point, is a nudist beach, Canada's first. So do the Musqueam object to the nakedness, right next to their reserve?

"Oh no," says Larry. "If people want to be without clothes, they can be. Traditionally, we would have been there in almost that state, because it's so hot. And we didn't have a Victorian attitude about the body, you have to remember that."

A century ago, the northern side of Wreck Beach and the beaches to the east—Spanish Banks and then Jericho and Locarno beaches—were salty marshland crossed by streams filled with pink and chum salmon and cutthroat trout and teeming with bird life. "There would have been high grasses all along there," Larry says. "A lot of that has been filled in, where the swampy areas were. It didn't have the clean sand before, a lot of that has been shipped in."

The Vancouver Park Board signed a hundred-year lease for the beaches with the province in 1929, and turned it into a playground of pristine sand, volleyball courts, parking lots and logs lined up in neat rows. Like Stanley Park, this once-rich ecosystem was transformed into a sterile, curated parkland, an artificial patch of "wilderness" for swimmers and daytrippers. And like Stanley Park, this former village site has been scrubbed of all traces of its Indigenous heritage, except for human remains that sometimes appear when luxury houses are being constructed on the bluffs overlooking the beaches. (In 2023, four of the ten most expensive houses in Canada were on Belmont Avenue over the beach; two more, including the most expensive, a three-lot concrete fortress built by Lululemon founder Chip Wilson and valued at seventy-three million dollars, were on nearby Point Grey Road.)

The other part of campus that has become important to Larry is the Indian Residential School History and Dialogue Centre, which opened in 2018. He likes to come here and take a break in the surrounding Library Gardens, a lush park of indigenous plants. Right now he's sitting on a wooden bench under a large cedar tree with a fine view of the stepped terraces and the elegant glass walls of the centre. To his left is the imposing bulk of Main Library, one of the few old buildings on campus, its neo-Gothic stone façade a symbol of the university.

"They declared this the middle of campus, right here; the president's office is right up there," he says, pointing to the Koerner Library building to the south. "To me, this has come to be a special spot."

The centre is the western repository of the archives of the Indian Residential School Commission, and Larry is pleased that survivors or their families can come here to research their stories. "It's good for anyone who becomes interested in residential school issues, not just students," he says. "What made them do this, why, how did it all come about? What were the results?"

Larry managed to avoid residential school, but many in the Musqueam community—including his wife—weren't so lucky. So what does the centre mean, to Musqueam and other First Nations, to all Canadians?

"Hopefully it means that people will become a little bit more aware of all the acts of denial created by the Canadian government. People say it was the church, when really it was the Canadian government. But also you have to remember, this is an English country. The crown of England adopted the Doctrine of Discovery [three fifteenth-century papal bulls] in 1763. The royal proclamation said, this land belongs to the Indigenous people. But the Doctrine of Discovery, which is a dehumanizing document, gives permission to all the European nations to go forward and appropriate lands that are not Christian. So North America and the rest of the world had to suffer under that.

"The Canadian government is an offshoot of the British parliament, and Britain is the heartland of freedom and democracy. Which had no problem subjugating Indigenous people as part of their colonialist system. It's important for students to understand the anomaly that is happening there; don't do as I do, do as I say. That was our hope anyway, when we agreed that there should be a western repository."

When he gives Musqueam land acknowledgments, Larry always welcomes people to "this unceded land." *Unceded* is a legal term many don't grasp, he says. "To cede land is to relinquish it or allow it to be sold. Our people have never sold our land, have never given up our land, and still have a claim in process. We have never lost it in a battle. And there is no agreement of occupation, none whatsoever. Britain has arbitrarily occupied the land. Canada has occupied the land. The province has occupied the land. The cities have occupied our lands, without agreement or remuneration to the First Peoples of this land. And that is led by now King Charles III, the new king of Britain, who is still the head of state in Canada and the head of our military."

This is true of most of what we now call British Columbia; about 97 percent of the land, an area greater than France and Germany combined, was seized in the late 1800s without a treaty or any attempt at a legal transfer of rights. The Indigenous inhabitants were considered a "vanishing race" who would soon disappear or be assimilated in the colonial tide.

"We are still a colonial country, even though Canada says that we have separated . . . The Crown of Britain is still the head of state. And the head of that state has the power to release the Indigenous Peoples from the Indian Act. The Crown has never done that. The late queen, just passed, in her reign for seventy years, had the opportunity, and would not allow Indigenous Peoples to be released from under the thumb of the Canadian government. We are still wards of Canada. Canada has a fiduciary obligation to take care of the First Nations of Canada, and it hasn't."

This whole history of settler colonialism has only become common knowledge in the last few years. "How many Canadian-born people know anything about it?" Larry asks. "Very few. It's a subject that's only now starting to be spoken of. It's a part of Canada's history that's still shrouded in the shadows. . . . If we have dialogue between international students that come from war-torn, politically subjugated countries, to this wonderful, free land, they can have a better understanding of that history."

"Today we have concrete," Larry adds. "We don't have any real forests. We don't have any salmon-bearing streams. We don't have plants for medicines or plants to make our homes. We have to import all of that from someone else's territory. That's part of the colonial system: you come in and you harvest everything and leave behind devastated people. That's how I feel: that it's progress, but it's not sustainable progress."

Larry notes the irony that the centre sits between the Koerner Library and the Irving K. Barber Learning Centre, both named after men who made their millions in forestry. "Barber made his fortune logging in the Kootenays, on unceded lands. . . . You know who the biggest benefactor of UBC is? It's not Koerner, it's not

Barber, it's not [Peter A.] Allard," the lawyer the UBC law school is named after. "It's Musqueam! The billions of dollars of real estate that have been appropriated, that Metro Vancouver and UBC sit on. And if you can't get that out of all of this, somebody has to wake you up!"

////////////////

From the Indian Residential School History and Dialogue Centre, we walk south down Main Mall as far as the Reconciliation Pole, an extraordinary and original work carved by Haida artist and hereditary chief 7idansuu, James Hart, who worked on it for more than two years, with a team of assistants plus guest artists from First Nations across Canada.

One of the largest poles ever raised in British Columbia, the massive Reconciliation Pole is 17 metres tall and 1.7 metres wide at the base, and weighs 12 tonnes. Hart helped select the tree, an eight-hundred-year-old western red cedar, on Haida Gwaii. The crew began the carving on the islands and finished it at UBC, in a carving shed by MOA.

Haida poles are read from the bottom up. The lower section, featuring salmon, a raven and a bear, symbolizes the time before contact. Then comes residential school, symbolized by two schools, carved separately and bolted on to either side of the pole, their straight lines standing out against the surrounding curves. Above them stands a row of children—carved by Coast Salish, Maliseet, Cree, Haida and Inuit artists—topped by parents in traditional dress hugging their children. Next up are two boats, to represent moving forward, travelling together into the future. On the very top of the pole is a massive eagle, its black wings outstretched.

"It's about power, determination," Hart told me at the time. "It's taking off into the future. I hope people get the meaning of it. We [Indigenous people] know about residential school, but it's for the rest of the country."

The pole shines with thousands of copper nails, each one representing a dead child. According to the Truth and Reconciliation Commission, at least six thousand children never returned from residential school—and recent discoveries of large unmarked grave sites suggests the number may be much higher. Like Larry, Hart was lucky, he says—he didn't go to residential school, though his grandfather, great-uncles and many other relatives and friends did.

Many people contributed to the pole project by hammering nails into it while it lay on site. "For the survivors, nailing in a nail makes them feel good," Hart says. "They remember their lost ones. . . . It's quite emotional."

Larry finds the finished pole emotional too, but he is still angry about the lack of consultation with Musqueam during the planning process. "The benefactor, Michael Audain, he's a real estate developer, but he's also an expert in Native art, so he knows about protocol. They commissioned the pole, to be raised on campus, and they didn't let us in on it. And when they did, they were already shipping it down for completion. We don't do poles here like this, we do house poles, single figure. When you look at this pole, it's a historical pole that tells a whole story. The Coast Salish people don't do that."

This botched process recalls nearly eight decades of the Museum of Anthropology ignoring Musqueam, on whose land it stands, in favour of the Kwak'waka'wakw from northern Vancouver Island and their spectacular cannibal masks and the Haida and other northern Nations with their grand totem poles, all inevitably centre stage in the museum—not to mention the Haida village and houses that stand behind it, a huge carving project overseen by celebrated Haida artist Bill Reid in the 1950s. MOA finally signed a memorandum of affiliation with the Musqueam in 2006, and the two have worked together on various projects since; visitors to the grand museum now arrive via xʷən̓iwən ce:p kʷθəθ nəẃeyəɬ—"Remember your teachings" or Welcome Plaza—featuring work by Musqueam artists Susan Point and Joe Becker.

Larry was one of many First Nations guests who spoke at the raising of the Reconciliation Pole, on Saturday, April 1, 2017. It was a beautiful spring day, and more than three thousand people had come to participate in the healing ceremony. Some guests spoke to the crowd but many more, like Larry, preferred to talk in the privacy of a tent reserved for residential school survivors and their families.

"I didn't nail a nail in," Larry says. "My wife went to the boarding school in Port Alberni, the residential school, so she gets quite sensitive, emotional, when we're around this stuff." A few days before the raising the couple came to see the pole being finished: "We were watching and there were about half a dozen residential school survivors. They didn't just nail one nail, they nailed about fifty each. We were standing there, saying, OK you guys, we'll come back. We never made it back, until it went up."

After many hours of speeches and preparation, the pole was raised at five pm, with many hundreds of people—First Nations and settlers, young and old, new immigrants and Indigenous Canadians, both authors of this book and their families—taking hold of five main ropes and slowly pulling the massive carving skywards, under the close supervision of five rope directors and master of ceremonies Gordie Russ.

"Michael, ease off a little there," Russ yelled. "Buddy, pull some more. Gently now. Take up the slack." Silence followed as the pole rose, slowly reaching higher and higher into the pale blue sky.

"Steady now," Russ cried as the seventeen-metre pole finally stood bolt upright, still wobbling slightly from side to side. Then sunlight glinted off the eagle perched on top, and the crowd let out a huge cheer. Silence descended and many eyes were wet in the solemn moments that followed.

Being part of the huge crowd, couples with small children, single people with coffees, elderly men and women in their Sunday best, Canadians of all origins and faiths bowing their heads together, was deeply moving. Just a symbol, sure, but a symbol that felt like a step towards reconciliation, all of us together.

For Larry, seeing the magnificent pole in a prime spot on campus, a permanent monument to the suffering of Indigenous people across Canada, was deeply cathartic. Still is, whenever he visits.

"It was a big deal," he says. "Consider the far-reaching effect residential school has. We were kind of upset at first, because we weren't involved, but after looking at it, I said, 'I don't care who the artist is, it's an amazing pole.' And then he [7idansuu] got different Indigenous groups to finish various parts; there's a Musqueam figure, by Susan Point. It's an amazing pole, it's really reflective of British Columbia and the territories.

"It's really great that it happened; we just felt that we should have been informed right away."

A lot has changed between Musqueam and UBC in the last ten, fifteen years, but for Larry, there's still a long way to go. The policies that govern the institution have to be edited to reflect the ninety-four calls to action in the Truth and Reconciliation Commission report, and adapted to respect the UN Declaration on the Rights of Indigenous Peoples, now part of BC law.

"It's a big change for the institution," Larry says. "They have to change their mindset. The old ways date back to the Doctrine of Discovery. A lot of old-school people have to rearrange their historical facts and actually talk about them. It's talking about them that I think is the reluctance. It's like self-condemnation."

"Because Canadians are used to thinking that we're the good guys?"

"Yeah, Canada is the good guys! It's hard, that self-reflective thing. I think that's the challenge with the school curriculum stuff; teachers are afraid to talk in case they say something wrong. Well, you find out pretty quick. And you won't be condemned for it, you'll be corrected. We all know that you only learn by making mistakes, going forward, saying OK, I made a mistake, let's back up and start over."

He's been looking far off into the distance, but Larry suddenly turns back and sees the Reconciliation Pole again. "Well, there it is," he says. "It's a beautiful pole. Big tree—it was nice seeing it lying down."

He points out one blurry figure of a child, a shadow figure standing among the other children on the pole. "There are so many children that were taken away and never came back and there's no record of them, what happened to them. It's not unfinished—it's that way for a reason. For basically, the unknown soldier.

"I remember when they first started talking about reconciliation, the residential schools, they started handing out money to the communities: 'Here's $1,500, to do something about residential school.' Ten communities got together, we had a language conference, because there was so little money. And I kept saying, we need to get all this money together and put it all into one pot across Canada and build a monument beside the unknown soldier in Ottawa representing Canadian residential school survivors, so that people from around the world who come to Ottawa can see a monument to the lost souls, the living dead, the walking dead who are out here and don't know who they are, where they come from, what they belong to."

He thinks that Canadians and visitors need to know that—need to understand that there are broken people all across this country who don't know where they come from, what their inheritance could be. "And Ottawa—that's where it should be, for the world to see. Not me, not you, the world! People say, 'You're thinking too big.' I don't think so.

"The unknown soldier is there, and that's the guys that were lost. To me, that's what this pole represents."

⁓⁓⁓⁓⁓

Five years after it was raised, on May 11, 2023, another sunny spring morning on campus, the Reconciliation Pole was finally finished. "Launched," as Larry put it. On its base sits a new artwork, a shiny bronze spindle whorl co-created by James Hart and Musqueam carver Kayám̓ Richard Campbell. Five metres wide, the spectacular disc features four large salmon carved by Campbell, representing the Salmon People, the Musqueam, on whose lands the pole stands. Its name, θəʔit, means *truth*.

Larry was one of many Musqueam people invited to the unveiling. Naturally, when he took the microphone, he reminded the assembled dignitaries, including the UBC president, of the unfortunate history of the pole. It took a while, he told them, but now it is truly anchored to Musqueam territory. Launched.

After the event was over and the crowd had gone their way, a few passersby came to spend time with the pole in the silence of the afternoon. The bronze was hot in the spring sunshine, and already decorated with a few bird droppings. "It'll turn turquoise in the sun and rain, like the roof of the Hotel Vancouver," said one elderly woman with a smile.

Three tiny shoes, a lone sandal and two striped sneakers, sat at the pole's base, next to a white rock with TRUTH written on it in blood-red paint.

Chapter Ten

Seeing Ghosts /
Home to China

"Man U, FA Cup champions!" says David, the welcoming guard at the Chinese Canadian Museum. David knows Larry well; they share a love for the English soccer team Manchester United, which Larry is showing off today in a stylish black-and-red jacket decorated with an embroidered version of the famous Man U "Red Devil" crest.

"I got it at the ferry terminal in Tsawwassen, on the way to Nanaimo," Larry explains later, when we're sitting out of the rain in the museum's guest room, under the watchful eyes of a giant handcrafted dragon head. We've come to the museum to meet with Sarah Ling, a friend and colleague of Larry's who's one of the founding curators of the stylish new museum, which opened last year in the Wing Sang Building, the oldest building in Chinatown. "My wife likes to shop around, and I needed a better rain jacket. Because of the connection with my half-sister, I thought I'd get this one."

Larry is talking about Yuk Ying, his father's daughter with his Chinese wife. It turns out that before he wed Larry's mother, Hong Tim Hing had been married in China in a traditional ceremony to a young woman from his home village, Sei Moon in

Guangdong province. And after his first son Gordon was born in Vancouver, his father had returned to China and spent a few months with his first wife. The result was Yuk Ying, who was born three months before Larry, making Larry his father's third child, not second. "No wonder I suffer from middle-child syndrome," he says. "I'm even more of a middle child than I thought."

Larry and his siblings found all this out in the late 1940s, a decade before their father died. Larry remembers the shock of reading his father's insurance papers and seeing a mysterious Chinese woman listed as his beneficiary. "Who the hell is this?" Larry asked his mum, but she shrugged it off. Seems she'd known, or sort of known, about her husband's bigamy for years.

"I say 'bigamy,' but that's just the Canadian legal term for it," says Larry. "In both cultures it was normal." He gestures to the museum's home, named after a wealthy merchant named Yip Sang who built it for his family of twenty-three children from four wives, three of whom had dominion over their own floor of the building.

His mum may have been accepting of this news, but Larry, who was a teenager when he heard it, was overcome with anger at his father. "I wasn't very happy at the way he treated my mother," he says, "in a physical sense. And how he never really helped us financially and was more interested in trying to make money by gambling." For the next two years, Larry didn't talk to him.

When the news came that Tim Hing was in hospital with cancer of the kidney and liver, Larry was still irked and slow to respond. After ten days, his mother said, "Y'know, your dad's family is askin' for you: Where is Number Two Son? You need to go, that's your father." Larry told her, "I cannot go because, in my mind, my father is not the person I believe he should be. I'm not going to go in there and talk to him just because everyone says he's dying." Sure enough, three or four days later Larry's father passed away, on November 1, 1956. He'd lived thirty-six of his fifty years in Canada.

The gravity of his actions didn't sink in until five years later, when Larry suddenly started crying one day. His wife asked him what the matter was, and he said, "My dad came to my mind and I just broke down." To this day, it's still an unresolved issue for Larry. "Every so often he comes to my mind, and he brings tears to my eyes—I can still cry over the thought of my father dying and me not resolving things prior to his death.

"The lesson for me was that I couldn't dictate to other people," Larry says. "He had his dreams, he had his faults, and I grew up to be a person like that also. I've had to deal with issues within our family, where the members have to be accepted *as they are*, because that's who they are. That's something I couldn't understand at that age, although I was supposedly a very mature person at twenty-one. I had some issues that I still deal with, and I don't have the answers—except that you need to be accepting of other people."

Larry and his siblings found out about their half-sister in the 1950s. But she became real to them in 2009, when Yuk Ying came to visit them in Vancouver from Manchester in England, where she lives. Widowed after the death of her first husband, a Chinese British man, she has three sons, two from her first marriage who immigrated to Australia and a third from her second marriage who lives near her in Manchester. Last Larry heard, his Mancunian nephew was running a fish and chips shop.

"Good occupation in Manchester."

"That's what I hear, they eat a lot of fish and chips there."

"About eight years later we lost track of her," Larry adds. "She used to contact Gordie's wife, they felt comfortable talking because they spoke the same dialect from the [Pearl] delta. Then she stopped communicating."

///////////////

For the Grants, the visit from Yuk Ying was just the first step in a process of reconnecting with the Chinese side of their family. They took a much bigger step four years later, when they began planning a family trip to Sei Moon to see the village where their father was born. At the last minute, they were joined by a two-person film crew who would document the journey in the award-winning documentary *All Our Father's Relations*.

The idea for the trip came from Edmond Leong, a Chinese cousin and friend who had grown up on the reserve with the family. He heard that a lot of Sei Moon was going to be bulldozed as part of a huge construction project and talked to Gordie, Larry's older brother, about it. "He said, you've got to come to China if you want to see your dad's village," Larry says, "because the government wants to punch a bullet train through there, they're going to destroy a whole bunch of houses. Gordie and I said 'We'll go' immediately.

"The thought of something we were connected to being demolished was the decider," Larry adds. "We knew our grandfather, knew that Dad went back and forth. We wanted to see it all before it disappeared."

The whole family had been reluctant to visit China for close to a century, a legacy of the Chinese Exclusion Act. Even after the 1960 amnesty, many Chinese immigrants and their families were afraid to go home because they didn't trust the Canadian authorities to let them back in. Larry's great-uncles and uncles had almost never dared, having risked and paid so much to come to Canada only to find themselves excluded from society, treated like second-class citizens, the "yellow peril."

The fear ran deep. "For many years, I never imagined going to my father's homeland," Larry's brother Howard says in the film. "I never spoke about it, never thought about it, never asked about it.... The fears from our uncles and great-uncles were ingrained. I was afraid to go, afraid I wouldn't be accepted. How would we communicate, would it be a hollow experience?"

On board from the start with Larry and Gordon were their wives, Gina and Jean, who did a lot of the organizing, with Jean doubling as the fourth translator because she had spent several years in a village near Sei Moon and spoke the local dialect. Larry's granddaughter Desirae and grandson Casey came too.

Up until the day of departure, people kept changing their minds. "Howard never gave an answer, he danced right around it," says Larry. "Decided to go last minute, with his eldest son, Wade." Their sister Helen changed her mind the other way, dropping out a few days before; Larry's grandson William did the same.

Sarah Ling, the film's lead producer, will never forget being at the airport with this great, excited clan, three generations of the Grant family about to set out on their adventure into the unknown. It was November 1, 2013, and as they waited for China Southern Airlines flight 330 for Guangzhou to depart, someone started singing "Happy Birthday" for Howard. It was also the fifty-seventh anniversary of Hong Tim Hing's passing, ninety-three years after he had left China on a steamer bound for Vancouver.

Sarah and the film's director, Alejandro Yoshizawa, had decided at fairly short notice to tag along. "Al and I thought it would be a great event to document, even just for family," she recalls. "We asked them all if they wanted to be recorded, and they backed it."

"We didn't have any money," she adds. "Most films like that are made on passion, you don't need glitzy equipment. We did minimal shooting. I held one camera at some points. Al and I wanted to just be flies on the wall, be respectful. We didn't want to interrupt."

As they approached the village, Edmond said, "Don't drive in, let's walk." So the whole hesitant clan got out of the car and started to amble onwards on foot. The entrance was marked by a striking, yellow-tiled gate, a workaday version of ornate ones like Vancouver's Millennium Gate, that sat in the middle of a traffic roundabout on the edge of town, with the village's name carved in green letters on a high stone plaque. Its construction had been funded by donations from all the great-uncles who had left for Canada.

"They raised money, pooled it and sent it back to the family in the village, to help them to erect a gate," Larry says. "Edmond was saying, your family put up that gate, we should walk through it." So they did, their backs to a concrete overpass, moving slowly down a narrow road past school kids in uniforms on their bikes and workers transporting firewood, the family house visible in the distance. High-pitched beeps made them step aside, and there was Larry's grandson Casey, sitting on the back of a motor scooter with a huge grin on his face; one of the villagers had recognized him and offered him a lift.

"That moment, my whole being said, 'I'm home,'" Larry says. "It really hit me that way. This is the other half of my life I had no idea about. My spiritual being became grounded at that moment, in that village." At age seventy-seven, he had come home to China, a mythical land ten thousand kilometres from Musqueam that he had only ever imagined.

///////////////

Fifty-seven years after his father's death, Larry walked into a tiny village in southern China and saw a ghost. A crowd of strangers surrounded them, greeting them in Cantonese and smiling happily. Many, they would soon learn, were close relatives—their father's family, brand-new faces that looked awfully like familiar faces they remembered from the farm.

"They were feeding us and introducing us to cousins, nephews and nieces that we had never met," says Larry, "when along comes an uncle I didn't know that I had! I was taken aback. Holy smokes. He was the spitting image of an uncle that had come to Canada and lived for twenty-plus years here before his death, Uncle Tommy. Here was this guy who looked like he stepped out of the grave. It was unbelievable."

The actual reunion only lasted a few hours, which went by in a blur. When they first saw their uncle, their father's youngest brother who looked like the long-lost twin of Uncle Tommy, Larry and his two brothers found it hard to speak. They just hugged him and drank tea and ate lunch together, while the framed photos of their common ancestors looked down proudly from the walls.

These relatives they'd never met knew who Larry and his siblings were; they produced photo albums with faded snaps of the Canadian family, including one of Uncle Tommy, and others of Gordon and Howard, back when he sported a handlebar moustache.

Larry was shown a journal written in Cantonese that recorded several centuries of his father's genealogy in China. "I was told,

'You are the seventeenth generation of this house,'" he recalls. "Oh my god. That was my reaction. Going there and being hugged and fed, it's not something in a book at that point. To be embraced and hear someone say, 'This is where you belong, this is where you come from' was very emotional." The words echoed the way Larry and his siblings had been welcomed into the home villages of their extended Musqueam family when they visited as kids, a big part of every summer.

"You could see so many memories flooding back," says Sarah. "I felt really privileged to be there. At one point I was sitting near Gordie and he was crying. It was really hard to leave the family, the visit was so short. And we were relying on translators."

"You could feel the emotion, see the emotion," interjects Larry. "You didn't need a translator, just being there made it so meaningful. It was much more emotional than I'd expected. Maybe because of our age. It was amazing to see the acceptance pouring out from our relatives." This was no "hollow experience"—they were being welcomed into the bosom of their long-lost family, their long-lost homeland.

"I was really happy then, while doing it, and after," says Larry. "Just being in China, the homeland of our *baba* and all our other ancestors. I had a hard time keeping my thoughts together."

///////////

It took Larry a long time to unpack all the emotions the trip sparked. Supporting Sarah and Alejandro while they spent the best part of three years making *All Our Father's Relations* helped.

Sarah grew up in Prince Rupert, with parents who emigrated from Guangdong, like Larry's father; she is now exhibition and collections manager at the Chinese Canadian Museum in

Vancouver, the first of its kind in Canada. She met Larry when she was a student at the University of British Columbia, doing a BA in English Literature with a minor in First Nations and Indigenous Studies; she later finished an MA in Interdisciplinary Studies. She attended all three levels of Larry and Dr. Patricia Shaw's hən̓q̓əmin̓əm̓ courses and they worked together on several language projects, including a children's book on Larry's life in three languages: English, Cantonese and hən̓q̓əmin̓əm̓. She lived for a while on the reserve and is close to a lot of his family, especially his sister, Helen. "She's like a niece to us," says Larry.

When they came back to Vancouver, the family and the film team had many meetings at Gordon and Jean's house, discussing the best way to tell the story of their parents' lives. "We wanted to educate Canadians about how families were shattered by these policies," says Sarah. Larry agrees: "All of those hardships that were endured by our ancestors, of not having parity, equality and equity in society—I would like the viewers to have a better understanding of that," he told an interviewer later. "A lot of things were said and done. But you just did your best. I just kept pushing and pushing."

Sarah and Alejandro ended up recording and piecing together hours upon hours of interviews, including some moving scenes where the family reminisces about the early days and talks about the trip while eating Chinese dinner with chopsticks at a long table at Gordon and Jean's house. These are interspersed with animated sections describing Agnes and Tim Hing's life on the reserve. By the time we get to Sei Moon, we know the family well and realize what's at stake.

The film premiered at the Vancouver Asian Film Festival to a sold-out crowd in November 2016, almost three years to the day after the trip—and sixty years after Hong Tim Hing's death. It moved a lot of people and was awarded Best Canadian Feature. It has been screened many times since, across Canada and internationally, including several times on CBC and BC's Knowledge Network. Sarah even went to Beijing for a screening there, largely on her own dime. "There was a lot of uptake from all directions, it became a really big and fun project," she says. "Much bigger than any of us expected."

Like most children of immigrants, Larry grew up with all kinds of preconceived notions about his father's homeland. In his mind's eye it was rural and not very sophisticated. He knew it was a small village surrounded by lush farmland and had seen the old photos of creaky windmills and barefoot children farming with water buffalo, but he was surprised to find that it was just like Musqueam: "The streets were paved, there was electricity, telephones," he says. "It was not third world."

Turns out that the Pearl River Delta is not just one of the lushest, most fertile areas on the planet; it's now also one of the most urbanized, a megalopolis of never-ending cities. Sure, they saw bright-green rice fields, but among a forest of cranes and tower blocks criss-crossed by highways and, these days, bullet trains. His father, who left rural China for opportunity in the West, would never have recognized the dynamic, industrial powerhouse the country has become. "Being there was a weird feeling!" Larry says.

Even weirder and more surprising was the intense emotional bond he felt to a land he had never visited and a people he had pretty much turned his back on as a child. "The reality of our connection really became apparent after watching the documentary multiple times," he says. "The emotions popped out, emotions that were always there, that I didn't recognize at first. It takes time for the walls to break down, walls that you've erected over all those years." Unlike Gordon, he hadn't cried when he was there, while it was all happening around him; it took repeated viewings of *All Our Father's Relations* to draw out the tears.

Why was the bond to his father's culture weaker than that to Musqueam? "Because it's your mother, your aunties who nurture you!" Larry says without hesitation. "That's true everywhere, in any culture. I've always been my mother's son, and my grandfather's grandchild." He has seen his Chinese uncles on and off all his life, but the bond didn't compare to the intense, cherishing embrace of his mother, the person who raised him and was always there. "She was the person who would pick me up from falling down and say, 'Is anything broken? No? Then go do it again!'" he says with a smile. Now, at age seventy-seven, he was having to recalibrate all this and open his heart to the Chinese side of his being.

Sarah also felt emotional watching the film, and it wasn't even about her village or family. "You don't get to process it until you're home," she says, "looking at footage again and again. When you're there you're just living it, it flies by. There is lots I forgot until I looked at the film."

"People cry when they watch it, people who have no connection to us or to China," Larry says. At first he was confused and wondered why. Now he thinks he understands; for a country like Canada, a nation of immigrants and nomads, people uprooted and replanted in a thousand myriad ways, "going home" is a universal longing, a fantasy we all dream but can never truly satisfy.

Larry is a vocal Chinese Elder today, a bridge between two communities, Asian and Indigenous, that have always shared many features. When he talks to Chinese Canadians or Indigenous students at UBC, or most anyone these days, he encourages them all to "Go home! Go visit the village your parents or grandparents came from, find out who they are, what it means, where your emotions lie. It will really assist you, make you more proud of who you are."

He has come to see that recognizing where your family comes from is so important. "Unless you're First Nations, you're here in a different land, far from the place of origin of your ancestors. You'll be surprised at the emotional connection that's there. It's completing the circle of your whole life, of who you are, what your origins are, the different communities you belong to. It's so, so important.

"Whether it's good or bad is not the issue, it's where your beginnings are. I've said that ever since, from watching the movie." So many Chinese Canadians have never been to China; so many Indigenous Canadians have never visited the place where their parents or grandparents grew up. "Because of my connection to China, my roots in Musqueam, I carry that history with me."

He acknowledges that not everyone will follow his advice, and tells the ones who do that they mustn't feel like they have to visit every relative or spend months or years learning the history or the language. Though some will.

"You will have your preconceived notions shattered. You don't need to stay, just go once and see home."

///////////////

One sunny afternoon while we're walking and talking by the river on the reserve, a tall Chinese man carrying a satchel who looks like a UBC student comes running up to Larry. He's breathless and obviously excited to have a moment alone with his teacher—and hero. He and Larry go into a huddle and he's soon on his way.

"A fan," says Larry, shaking his head. Amused but also a little flattered.

He explains that a lot of the Chinese students at UBC are fascinated by him because of his mixed Chinese and Indigenous ancestry. "They're not aware of Indigenous people being here in Canada because it is not part of the publicized image of the country," he says. "There's very little mention of us in the Canadian concept around the world. They don't know we're here."

"When they're trying to attract international students or immigrants, that's not something they focus on?"

"No. They don't stress that. But also, the question always pops up, 'How is it that you're an Indian but you're not from India? You're from Canada.'"

"So what do you answer?"

"The government declared us Indian."

"Columbus being lost."

"Yeah, Columbus being lost in the ocean, found by the people of Canada today."

///////////

For his whole life, Larry never denied being part Chinese. All the people he and his siblings dealt with over the years thought of them that way. "But inside I was Musqueam, still am," he says. And not knowing the homeland, the lands his ancestors walked upon and came from, survived and flourished in, stopped him from truly embracing that part of his heritage. Until he went home.

"It's part of you, as every person who comes from a place knows," Larry says. "Going there opens up your mind. Completely. About how much of me is part of that land, whether I live there or not. Part of my soul is forever there, walking where my father walked, where his father raised him, where all those generations walked.

"It's very much how we were taught in Musqueam," he adds. "This is where you come from, this is where you belong. That same revelation happened over there, opened our minds: 100 percent acceptance of being Chinese.

"I can make myself cry thinking about it," he says, smiling all the while.

Chapter Eleven

From Student to Teacher /
In the Classroom in Musqueam

The 22nd of April 2024 is a luminous spring day. After months of cold and incessant rain, the sun is finally shining brightly at the mouth of the Fraser River. Not a breath of wind stirs the tall grasses by the water's edge. The only sounds come from birds in the poplars and guests arriving for the annual hənq̓əmin̓əm̓qən ct ce? ʔɬyəs tə n̓ a weyəl ʔəm̓i le? ʔəɬtən—Musqueam Community Potluck and Year-End Celebration—parking their cars next to the Musqueam Cultural Centre, at the southern tip of the reserve.

Originally erected in downtown Vancouver as the Four Host First Nations Aboriginal Pavilion for the 2010 Winter Olympics before being reassembled here, the cultural centre is a spectacular building. In the shape of a traditional Coast Salish hat, its cedar walls and roof are circular, reaching up to a pitched round opening in the centre of the ceiling. On the south side, floor-to-ceiling glass panels look out on the broad river just before the spot where it meets the vast expanse of the Pacific Ocean.

Inside, Musqueam band members are arriving with their arms full of home cooking. The folding tables are lined with metal pans of turkey and stuffing, BBQ salmon, mashed potato, Brussels sprouts and steamed vegetables. Coffee, juice and an array of desserts sit near the far door, open to the grassy expanse and the river and sky beyond.

An elderly Musqueam woman wearing a spectacular woollen jacket with a fur collar and traditional floral decoration tap-taps her way in and greets some friends and family at a table in the centre. One of them is Helen, Larry's sister, whose smile is illuminated by sunlight beaming through the round hole at the top of the radial cedar roof. All around the women, the walls are adorned with bright woollen hangings in Musqueam patterns, many featuring canoes and paddles or sʔiːɬqəẏ, the doubled-headed serpent whose droppings gave birth to the məθkʷəẏ plant and people.

As the guests file in, they are welcomed by today's MC, Larry, resplendent in a pink dress shirt topped with a black felt waistcoat with a Musqueam border embroidered for him by his stepdaughter, plus a jade tooth on a leather strap dangling around his suntanned neck. Maybe it's the hopeful spring weather or the microphone he's holding, but he looks young and sprightly. Tanned and smiling, a microphone in one hand, his greying hair wavy and long, he could pass for an aging rock star, a Musqueam Mick Jagger: "My wife doesn't like it, wants me to cut it off!" he says with a grin.

Larry has good reason to be proud. After a few weeks' delay caused by a series of deaths in the community, today is graduation day. The students of First Nations and Endangered Languages 102: Introduction to a Salish Language II: hən̓q̓əmin̓əm̓ (Musqueam language) and FNEL 202 Intermediate Salish Language II: hən̓q̓əmin̓əm̓ (Musqueam language) are set to give their final presentations before a casual gathering of happy Musqueam band members, including several Elders and hən̓q̓əmin̓əm̓ speakers. The students are easy to identify: a diverse mix of keen language learners, about a quarter of them Musqueam, they are all wearing matching jet-black t-shirts printed with "hǝṅq̓ǝmiṅǝm̓" in bright white lettering.

"The students make two- to three-minute videos or animations these days," Larry explains with a nod. "Makes it interesting. A lot of them know the technology, how to make little films. Everything in hǝṅq̓ǝmiṅǝm̓, of course."

The first group of beginner students takes the floor. They show a short animation introducing the game show they've made, about addition and subtraction. Then one learner asks for a volunteer from the audience to compete with him; the first to guess the answer has to punch the rubber chicken (kʷawʷǝt tǝ čǝlǝkǝns in hǝṅq̓ǝmiṅǝm̓) lying on a table between them and shout the answer out. Giggles follow, then raised hands. The math is easy but the pronunciation hard. More giggles, more volunteers, faster and funnier squeaks as the calculations flash up on the screen and the volunteers bash the rubber chicken in glee.

The tone's been set; this is fun, the audience wants to join in, and hey, these students can pronounce those tough hǝṅq̓ǝmiṅǝm̓ words better than expected. Larry reminds people to get seconds of food or have some dessert and introduces the next group, two young women who have created five versions of the kids' song "Head, Shoulders, Knees and Toes," using the hǝṅq̓ǝmiṅǝm̓ words for various body parts: heads, shoulders, knees, toes, but then skin, brains, heart, hair, belly. "Bear with us, it was hard to squeeze all these syllables into the melody," says one of the students. She leads the sing-a-long and the whole gathering joins in, young and old, the elderly women who've done this before with their grandchildren especially loud and giggly, their happy voices filling the vast space with a joyful celebration of their ancestral language.

////////////////

Larry came late to language teaching. In 1998, the year before he retired from four decades as a tradesman, his family, especially his younger brother Howard, encouraged him to enrol in the hən̓q̓əmin̓əm̓ language program that was being developed by the University of British Columbia and Musqueam at the time, so he started attending Linguistics 100 and First Nations Language Group 100B. "The language program just grew into something that awakened memories from my childhood," he says. "That's what's been occupying my life in the last twenty years, the hən̓q̓əmin̓əm̓ language and the desire to reawaken it within our community."

Rediscovering a half-forgotten language after all that time was a strange, complicated experience, one that slowly rebuilt his connection to the faraway world of his mother and her upbringing in another century, when everyone spoke hən̓q̓əmin̓əm̓ and saw life through that lens. From the age of fifteen he had rarely spoken his mother tongue, though he was exposed to hən̓q̓əminəm̓ and hul̓q̓umín̓um̓, the Vancouver Island dialect, through events at the Big House: spirit dancing, namings, memorials, funerals. "The language was always spoken then and that kept it alive in my memory," Larry says. "I'm aware of that now, something that I thought was long gone is still there and has slowly come back.

"The words come out of my memory, even now, without me thinking about them," Larry explains. "And you say, 'Oh, I remembered something.' It's like opening up an old, old book, and you think, I remember that. She used to say that."

He was part of a cohort of Musqueam students who went through four years, four levels, of language classes together.

"They were just being created, and I got more and more linguistic jargon and analysis, morphology and phrenology. I was the old man in the class all the way through. Some were twenty years old, some in their thirties."

"You must have been a pain to teach."

"Oh yeah, I was always correcting students," he says, half ashamed, half proud. Soon he was correcting the teacher too, especially when she had the gall to call the Musqueam language a "dialect."

"Our own people say this is our language, hən̓q̓əmin̓əm̓; the linguists spell it Halkomenem; the Island dialect is hul̓q̓umín̓um̓ or Hulkomenum; the Upriver dialect is halq̓eméylem or Halkomelem. Linguists say it's a dialect, our people say it's a language. Why would I speak your language in my house? When I'm doing my work? Can you tell me that? We're here in BC, no one speaks French in an English-speaking house and no one speaks English in a French-speaking house. Why are we any different? So that was always a bone of contention."

Eventually they settled this by asking him to co-teach the courses, which he now does with linguistics PhD candidate Fiona Campbell, "an academic Canadian girl from the Kootenays."

The founder and first professor of UBC's First Nations and Endangered Languages program, Dr. Patricia Shaw, insisted on hiring Larry, a retired auto mechanic with a high-school certificate, as a prestigious adjunct professor, not a sessional instructor, the usual first step for a non-academic lecturer. She had to twist the rules and lean on the faculty to get this approved, but the principle was important; she believed his ancestral knowledge should be given the same recognition as the theoretical expertise of his new colleagues. Larry is still grateful. "She was the driving force, still is pretty well," he says. "She told me, the knowledge you carry, nobody else carries that—it's at that level."

For Larry, speaking hən̓q̓əmin̓əm̓ is "just doing stuff that was taught to me by my mum, mostly, and other women." Men taught him how to work and survive in Musqueam and beyond, while women talked about history, genealogy, tradition. "A lot of it is overhearing discussions, kitchen table talk, having bread and jam at the end of a meal, just talking, recounting history, stories, ceremonies." Top of the list was his grandfather Seymour's sx̌ənəq (potlatch), which his mother always spoke about: "Remember where you come from, he's the guy that did that." That gave Larry and his family stature in Musqueam, but also when they visited other communities Seymour was connected to, their extended families on Vancouver Island and across the border in Washington state.

Larry sees other Musqueam going through the same journey he has been on. "As our young people gradually mature—or grow older, whichever comes first," he says with a chuckle, "they will begin to understand how important our language is, to exactly who we are." Twenty years studying and teaching the language has only reinforced the value hən̓q̓əmin̓əm̓ has to community self-worth, identity, kinship, culture, history.

///////////////

Linguists estimate that the world's eight billion people speak about seven thousand unique languages, distinct from all the dialects and local varieties. Up to half of these are likely to disappear within the next few centuries as technology reaches deeper into our lives and its dominant languages overwhelm the unique and particular. Just 4 percent of the world's population now speaks 96 percent of its languages, mostly in forgotten recesses of the globe. In the Americas, where English, Spanish and Portuguese are juggernauts crushing all before them, the holdouts are concentrated in cloudy valleys in the highlands of Guatemala and the Andes and the rainforests of the Amazon. And in British Columbia, a wild hinterland that's home to thirty-four distinct Indigenous languages, more than half of the total in Canada. Only three Indigenous Canadian languages—Cree, Anishinaabemowin and Inuktitut—are still spoken by more than a few thousand people. Like most of the fifty-five others, hən̓q̓əmin̓əm̓ is classified as Severely Endangered by UNESCO.

Linguists estimate that a language dies every three months, never to be spoken again. It's hard to fathom what that loss means. In the words of anthropologist Wade Davis, "an old-growth forest of the mind" is erased forever. The Musqueam's last true first-language speaker passed away in 2002, so Larry and the team at UBC and Musqueam are mostly learning from archives these days, listening to and making recordings and expanding the dictionary. For a few years there were still a few silent speakers left, people who knew a lot of phrases or words but were not able to carry on a conversation. "They would sit and listen for hours and never speak," Larry says, like sailors marooned in a fog, knowing the land is close but not being able to see it or set foot onshore. "Even myself, I get like that sometimes."

The challenge now is trying to create everyday language out of transcripts, recordings and videos, something academic linguists don't do; they focus on grammar, not banter. "First you have to learn the language, then you can riff on it," Larry explains. "Linguists aren't interested in, 'Hey buddy, how's your girlfriend? How you doin'? What the hell you up to? Holy smoke, ya loser.' They're not interested in that stuff, they want to know the grammatical speech. So the semantics, the everyday stuff, you have to work that out yourself."

Learning a language few people speak is challenging, especially one so different from English. Larry believes the only way is hands-on learning. He uses the example of chopping wood with a student, while getting them to talk about the various actions: you get the wood, buck it up, split it. "In hən̓q̓əmin̓əm̓ there's terms like 'compact the wood,' it's quite different from English. Because it's a polysynthetic language," meaning words have many compounded variants, to the point where you're speaking in one-word sentences.

"You also have all kinds of affixes you can add to words," continues Larry, "and sentences are constructed verb-subject-object, unlike English, which is subject-verb-object. Then you can add prefixes, suffixes, infixes; and there are re-duplications, for progression, ongoing. Diminutivization, pluralization. And there's different patterns, sometimes there's an L infix that gives you the pluralization, other times you have to use re-duplication. That kind of throws everyone off when they're learning. They get confused about what word means what. It's hard to pick up."

⁂

One day when he was deeply engrossin in language study, Larry realized that he had a mental block. Every time he tried talking, he'd get to a certain point and the words would dry up, so he'd stop talking hən̓q̓əmin̓əm̓ and revert to English.

Why? He has asked himself again and again, and can only guess at an answer, probably linked to his complicated childhood moving between cultures. "I stopped speaking hən̓q̓əmin̓əm̓ because my dad was upset that I could respond to it more than I could to Cantonese," he says. "In the house, arguing with my mother, he was really upset, he wanted her to stop speaking hənq̓əmínəm̓ to me."

At that time, in the thick of World War II, all Larry saw was war propaganda, cowboy movies: "the Canadian mindset, to belong, to be a hero, to be a leader. The Japanese were bad guys, the Indians were bad guys; all the heroes were white guys, all the victorious guys were white guys, everybody at school spoke English."

So he made a deliberate choice to turn the page, throw hənq̓əmínəm̓ away, let it go. He'd never asked himself why until he was sitting in class at UBC, a sixty-three-year-old "mature" student surrounded by wide-eyed twenty-year-olds asking him why he'd stopped speaking his own language. "I really regretted that after everyone in the class started asking," he says, his head bowed in resignation and a little bit of shame. "Why did I let it go? That's who I am."

Because he voluntarily stopped speaking hənq̓əmínəm̓, and hadn't spoken it for close to fifty years, he felt uncomfortable using his mother's language for a long time, even though he knew the words. "It's like I stopped singing, because of my life situation at the time," he says. "Now I'm trying to sing, and I'm having a really, really hard time. It's like throwing away a gift and then trying to bring it back, and you are not able to because your mind says it's gone. It's so challenging."

He may be one of the best hənq̓əmínəm̓ speakers alive, but Larry is well aware that he hasn't studied the language enough to truly master it. "You keep repeating the words over and over again—there are about ten thousand words—so that you actually become comfortable with different versions of lots of activities, all of the different versions of the root words. Every root has half a dozen variations."

That said, when Larry speaks it, he feels like he is reaching back to his mother and her parents and grandparents behind them, and how they spoke to him and her. The first time he spoke publicly in hən̓q̓əmin̓əm̓ he heard her voice, her presence: "The words that were coming out of my mouth were actually coming out of my mother, it was such an emotional thing. It made me understand how connected I was to my mother and to my mother's people."

"Sometimes I'm caught unawares," he adds. "It comes out, and it's like, I'm thinking about the syntax, overthinking it maybe, and the words are there, new words sometimes—I'm trying to keep it focused in a hən̓q̓əmin̓əm̓ way. And then it stops."

As a young man he remembers hearing great orators make speeches in hən̓q̓əmin̓əm̓ and he dreams of that happening again. "I could just see some of our young people standing there and talking and talking, telling history as the orators I knew did," he says. "And actual conversations fell out of my head, from those old people of my grandparents' era . . . how intelligent our people were to have developed a language as sophisticated as hən̓q̓əmin̓əm̓ without using any books or language schools."

"The denigration of Indigenous language and culture has been going on in this part of Canada for a hundred and fifty years now," Larry continues. "It's embedded in the loss of self-worth, self-identity, spirituality, all being discarded by colonial ways. It's unknowingly embedded in our psyche, which is a barrier that to some is insurmountable. They're embarrassed about sounds in their own languages."

When Larry was growing up, a few people in the community also spoke Chinook, a pidgin trade jargon used up and down the coast, like Swahili in East Africa, so that different groups who spoke wildly different languages could make themselves understood. It had a simplified grammar and only a few hundred words, and was mostly spoken by men who worked with other Nations, often far from home. "My uncle Sammy, my mum's brother, worked from southern Washington, near Oregon, all the way up to the Aleutian Islands off Alaska, fishing and logging," Larry says. "He spoke it. Mum didn't, Grandpa would have. It depended on who you had to talk to."

To Larry, English is no longer a language, it's a mishmash of Anglo-Saxon, Latin, French, tech code speak and words imported from all the colonies the British once ruled. "It's the world's trade jargon," he says with a smile. A poor person's Chinook.

////////////

"Do you play baseball?" asks Larry.

"Not for a long time, but I used to."

"A ball's coming at you today: what do you do?"

"Catch it."

"Why? Why do you catch it in a particular way?

"Muscle memory?"

"Yeah. You know where it's going, you know where it's going to land, and you know how to catch. Been awhile, but it's still there."

We're sitting in a diner in Chinatown drinking green tea, and I've just apologized for my appalling pronunciation of the word *haṅ́qəmiṅ́əṁ*. Again.

"Your mouth is locked in a ball," continues Larry. "That's what's wrong with adult language learners. They don't know how to open up that ball. Little kids—they don't know where the door is to that ball, so they take it in. Gulp." He gulps like a guppy.

Larry uses this metaphor to encourage his students to develop new muscle memories in class, learn new ways to make sounds. He wants them to understand the challenge, and the goal. "When I trip over and I'm falling, I know how to roll," he continues. "I did a lot of gymnastics in school and learned to roll. It's there. I don't know why. I've tripped and I've rolled over many times." We learn to speak a language the same way we learn a sport, by practising new actions again and again until they become instinctual.

This is hard to do when you have very few people to speak to. Larry can't speak hənʼqʼəminʼəmʼ at home—his wife is a survivor of Alberni Residential School and doesn't like him speaking the language around the house, as it brings back painful memories. When she went into the school she spoke the Island dialect, her father's tongue, and Nuu-chah-nulth, her mother's tongue. "Coming out of there, she could not speak, would not speak, either language, only English, because of the punishment she had for using the Native languages. To this day it's a really sad, sad thing."

Larry does talk with Fiona Campbell, his co-teacher, but they can only discuss very basic things because she's not Musqueam and only has an elementary-school understanding of the language.

"There's a couple of people I talk to," Larry continues. "My co-worker Vanessa and a couple of other staff members. Right now it's a really critical moment, to try and build up that confidence. I have had I don't know how many hundred Musqueam students through, and how many hundred UBC students, and the youth are beginning to speak out a little, more and more now."

Sometimes it catches him by surprise; he'll be walking down the street on the reserve and someone passing by will say, "ʔiʔə cxʷ ʔew

ʔəẏ ʔaɫ" ("How are you?") or "ctetəm čxʷ tə n̓a weyəl" ("What are you doing today?"). Those little moments are so satisfying.

"That used to be kinda normal when we were kids. We'd reply in English," Larry says with a shake of the head. "So it's challenging, trying to move back and remember the words, how to formulate the sentences. Once you learn the patterns, you're able to use them, because most of our words are verb words, which have all of these variations, the majority of which can be transformed into nouns."

Sometimes Larry feels as if his grandparents are making him stay in the language. He can't walk away from the teaching now, it's part of his life. "It's a very, very strange feeling, something I don't have control over," he says. "It's as if I need to teach someone else this language, and have to relearn as much as I can about it and push it forward. That's something that I had no intentions of doing when I first signed up."

"My hope is to one day hear our Musqueam language spoken at all community functions, have it re-introduced as the language spoken within the Musqueam Big House and as an everyday form of speech," Larry says.

"When called upon to publicly welcome people to Musqueam traditional ancestral territory I use our language as much as possible in the hopes that one day a young person will be the one speaking it."

//////////

Back at the Musqueam Community Potluck, three ungainly students have taken the stage. "We're going to sing a new version of 'Stand By Me,' the Ben E. King song," one explains. "I bet you know it—but not in hən̓q̓əmin̓əm̓!"

The music kicks in and the trio start belting their lungs out, pointing at the lyrics on a screen and gesturing for everyone to join them. "Please sing along, we'll be less embarrassed!"

Larry and his sister and the other Musqueam Elders stand up one by one and all join in, huge smiles on their faces.

Chapter Twelve

The Meaning of Home / In leləm̓

The sign on the fence in front of the development calls leləm̓ "An Urban Village in Pacific Spirit Park." Its name is adapted from the hən̓q̓əmin̓əm̓ word for *home,* leləm̓, inspiring the other marketing catchphrase, "The Meaning of Home."

"Rooted. Layered. Storied," reads the website for the second phase of the development. "Live in a place layered with the richness of community and nature. Rooted in the Musqueam way of life, edge way at leləm̓ is a refined collection of homes, steps from Pacific Spirit Park and the University of British Columbia. This boutique community is immersed in the tranquility of forest and sea, yet close to daily conveniences and premier schools. Discover a world beyond yourself and weave your own beautiful story here."

The first phase of leləm̓ was all sold out by the time it opened in June 2023, and it's impressive. Sitting right on the edge of UBC's main campus, the development was carved out of 7.3 hectares of forest land awarded the Musqueam in the 2007 deal that also gave them control of the University Golf Course it faces across University Boulevard. It includes two twenty-storey apartment towers, an array of low-rise townhouses and a commercial area built around a plaza and a high-end supermarket, Urban Fare.

Polygon Homes, the development company run by art collector Michael Audain of Reconciliation Pole fame, has done a fine job with the buildings, whose cedar entranceways and concrete features are elegant and seductive. A pharmacy and dentist have just opened and the restaurant, Wildlight Kitchen + Bar, was recommended in the 2023 and 2024 Michelin Guide. By the time the whole development is built out in nine years' time, it will be home to about two and a half thousand people in more than a thousand townhouses, condos and rental apartments.

"We got this land returned to us more than fifteen years ago," Larry says. As ever, he's wearing his Native Pride ballcap, standing in front of a spectacular house post decorated with a carving of a heron. Planning began the year after, with a lot of head-scratching. What to do with this block of rezoned land ripe for development? The band couldn't add it to the reserve, a complicated process that can take decades. It took five or six years to agree on the best way forward.

The result was the Musqueam Capital Corporation (MCC), a new economic development arm for the band separate from the Musqueam administration. It has a board of directors, most of whom are non-Indigenous and have experience in finance and real estate. Their mandate is to oversee development projects to supply resources to Musqueam. leləm̓ is a test case, the first of several major projects in the works.

"The whole concept did not exist before," Larry explains. "We had no economic development program, other than rental land. For years we had a chief who wouldn't enter into this sort of deal. 'Why buy back what's already ours?' he used to say."

Larry stops to look at the community centre, a soaring, 15,000-square-foot building about to open that will include a gym, a fitness centre, a childcare centre and various communal meeting spaces. "It's not just towers, it's a whole, inclusive community," he says. "That's basically how Musqueam has always looked at this kind of larger development. A pharmacy, a playground, a school, a coffee shop. A self-contained community that also has access to 10th Avenue and UBC."

"I've been to the supermarket, I can't afford to shop there myself," I add. "I live nearby, but I guess I'm not the target market."

"Me neither," says Larry with a laugh. "I don't get any higher than Stong's," a local supermarket. "It's aimed at UBC faculty, they're very short of faculty housing on campus." Accommodation is available for Musqueam band members, but even with the discounts they receive, it's too expensive for most.

"This is a cedar house post," Larry says, pointing to one side of a high arch between two buildings as we walk underneath it. A striking carved figure is holding a shield decorated with intertwined salmon; his legs are covered by a wonderful abstract fantasy reminiscent of a butterfly flapping its wings.

"Should we worry about the cracks?"

"No, the back is all reinforced behind here, they appear because the outside of the log dries too fast. In twenty, thirty, forty years it'll come back, it kind of neutralizes, in terms of water content."

"Is one side supposed to be higher than the other?"

"Yes, the high end is the front, and that's the back. The front figure would be facing the river, or the way you would come in or out of the community. Normally you would arrive by canoe.

"It's all Musqueam art. That's part of the branding, the marketing. We're trying to do that with all the developments we're involved in.

"Land development is a very strange concept," Larry continues, "because you're buying or leasing land. That's not an Indigenous value, we always focus on community stuff. We didn't have the development expertise, and that's the really hard thing to push, to go and get an MBA so you can really work with land development. Because that's all we have, all of our resources have been occupied or stolen by the Brits, Canada, BC. There's no other way for our community to be self-sustaining, except to go into real estate."

Projects like these are long term and demand patience. You have to invest a lot of money up-front and then wait for years before you start getting a return on investment. Musqueam was helped by a low-interest loan from the federal government's Canada Mortgage and Housing Corporation to support the cost of building rental homes as part of leləm̓.

"We're hoping the turnaround is less than twenty years," Larry says with a chuckle. "Like any development that's starting, you have to be careful with the seed money, it can take many years to make a profit. The community is always frustrated, because like most Indigenous communities, we're cash-poor, resource-poor, for our own housing. The budget report shows X amount, we've got millions of dollars, where is it? Why can't I have it, I want to buy a new truck! They say, it's invested. We're like farmers, we're land-rich but money-poor." It might be another generation before people start to reap the benefits, but as a business venture it seems to be the right move at the right time.

"This is new to me," Larry says, stopping to look up at a soaring condo building, an elegant, twenty-one-storey brown and yellow tower that's about to open; workers are busy removing a fence in front and cleaning up the entryway. A sign tells us it's

"West Wind," featuring one-bedroom apartments from $873,000; the three-bedroom townhouses that line it on either side start at $1,598,000. Serious money, even for Vancouver's pricey West Side.

"I can't believe how quick this is coming up," Larry says. "Some is the original construction; the church there." He points towards the pyramid-shaped roof of St. Anselm's Anglican Church, a graceful stone and wood structure built in 1953. "This is spipəy̓cəs, Crooked Branch Road. We named all these roads, this one is the curving shortcut between University Boulevard and Acadia Road. I'm impressed how quickly it's come up, and it doesn't look like they are cutting any corners."

Larry starts answering a question about long-term cash flow for the community—"Yes, it should be sustainable, hopefully"—but is drowned out by the roar of a digger careering down Acadia Road towards us.

"Careful, I don't want to be responsible for my co-author being run over by a front-end loader."

⁂

leləm̓ is the first of a handful of developments MCC has in the works. "There's Heather Lands, where the RCMP academy used to be," says Larry, referring to an 8.5-hectare chunk of land between 33rd and 37th avenues by Heather Street, near Queen Elizabeth Park in central Vancouver. "That's the three Nations," the Musqueam, Squamish and Tsleil-Waututh (MST), Vancouver's three original inhabitants, who bought 50 percent of this piece of under used Crown land in 2014 and are developing it with the Canada Land Company, a federal Crown agency that owns the other half. The city fast-tracked rezoning for development in 2022 so construction could begin in 2025.

In September 2024, BC Premier David Eby held a press conference with MST to announce that all 2,600 residences in Heather Lands would be sold at 40 percent off their market value, through a long-term loan system. "It's truly innovative and a uniquely Indigenous approach to development," Squamish councillor and spokesperson Sxwíxwtn Wilson Williams told the CBC. "We're opening up our lands to support the culture and economic sustainability of our people, but also to help provide housing in a city that is desperate for more."

But the most ambitious and controversial development is Jericho Lands, another MST–Canada Land Company co-production that's five times bigger than leləm̓ and still years from breaking ground, though it was unanimously approved by Vancouver city council in January 2024. It will transform a huge, thirty-six-hectare site near Jericho Beach on Vancouver's prosperous West Side that's currently home to little more than a posh private school, a small army barracks and a lot of grass into a forest of towers and townhouses. By the time it's built out in twenty-five to thirty years, it'll be home to twenty-four thousand people, more than the entire population of the adjacent neighbourhood of Point Grey today.

Local residents are incensed by this massive urbanization in the heart of a sleepy, affluent area next to a beloved green space, Jericho Park, and the even-more-beloved beaches of Locarno, Jericho and Spanish Banks. But Larry isn't moved by their complaints, which isn't surprising given the relentless urban and industrial development his people have been subject to on their traditional territory over the last two centuries—including those very beaches, where his ancestors once had a village with a burial site. "Maybe in our grandchildren's generation they'll be reaping the benefits of the things we gave up to get there," he says.

And do the three Nations, whose relationship is often acrimonious, find it easy to work together on these projects? "The developing consortium are not at each other's throats," Larry says diplomatically; "however, vocal band members will have their say and sometimes create dissension because of that. But this is a business partnership. It's got nothing to do with land claims."

The Musqueam won't just make money out of real-estate development. leləm̓ is largely subcontracted out, but the new jobs at MCC are providing invaluable business training. One recipient of this is Larry's granddaughter Desirae Fraser, who has a certificate in project management and started working with MCC while she was studying urban land economics at UBC Sauder School of Business. She is now working with Isthmus, a consulting firm that advises MCC on business development.

"If we take care and learn on the job, as time goes by, we can be self-sufficient in developing," Larry hopes. "So it's jobs and self-sufficiency. Develop that land and incorporate as many of our band members as possible in the process: trades training, business training.

"And for the future generation, taking care of our resources and looking after our people—that's what it's *really* about. We don't have any other real sources of income. Well, we have some, but real estate development, land development, seems to be the avenue we need to travel upon now.

"We also need politicians in the federal government," Larry adds. "We need that kind of training so we're not dependent upon others for that expertise." His nephew Wade Grant's election as a federal Liberal MP in April 2025 should help in that regard.

///////////////

The high-pitched sounds of children playing tells us we're now close to Norma Rose Point School, a primary and middle school next to leləm̓ that was rebuilt in a seismic upgrade completed in 2014. "Norma Rose Point was Musqueam," Larry explains, "our education coordinator and part of our original language community. She did so much, at UBC, the Vancouver School Board, the Richmond School Board—she was everywhere. Her primary concern was the betterment of Musqueam students."

All this without being a native hən̓q̓əmin̓əm̓ speaker; Point was "a married-in lady," a Stó:lō woman from up the Fraser Valley who became very prominent in the community for advocating education. When the school board renovated the building and decided to change its name from University Hill, they had a naming contest and Musqueam put her forward.

"It was accepted after a lot of discussion," says Larry. "A *lot*," he repeats with a laugh.

"You say that politely. Did they want to name it after Winston Churchill?"

"Or another Trutch, yeah," he replies, referring to Sir Joseph William Trutch, BC's first lieutenant governor, whose aggressively anti-Indigenous policies included reducing the size of many reserves by up to 90 percent; Victoria, Richmond and Vancouver have all recently renamed Trutch streets, the last, in Kitsilano, to šxʷməθkʷəy̓əmasəm ("Musqueamview Street"). The new signs are sitting in Larry's office on the reserve waiting to be installed, because Canada Post is having trouble working out how to process the hən̓q̓əmin̓əm̓ orthography in their automated sorting machines.

"Also, we want to put up signboards, explaining the name change, who Trutch was and what he did, and why his name has been dropped," says Larry. "We don't want to forget the history, we want to talk about it openly."

This reminds Larry of the first time the Musqueam were asked to rename a school, in Richmond in 2000. This was before they had finalized their own orthography, but despite the Latin spelling, the school board was still not happy with the proposed name: Spul'u'kwuks Elementary.

"There was an old village there, near Terra Nova Cannery," Larry says. "So we named it Spul'u'kwuks, 'bubbling water.' They wanted a name that was easier, do this, do that. No. That's the name of the village right there: Spul'u'kwuks." One parent complained bitterly to the CBC that the new name was unpronounceable, but it stuck.

/////////////////

Larry retired as a longshoreman in 1999, but at age eighty-eight, when most men are watching game shows on TV or sipping fruity drinks on a beach, he is working more than ever. He is Elder-in-Residence at the University of British Columbia's First Nations House of Learning. He is a Faculty Fellow at St. John's College; the inaugural Honorary Life Fellow at Green College; and Elder-in-Residence at the Justice Institute of British Columbia, where he works to "Indigenize" the curriculum for first responders and other workers who come into regular contact with First Nations people. For his day job, full-time five days a week, he is interim manager of the Musqueam Language and Culture Department.

Recognition for his extraordinary cultural knowledge has come, though late in life. In 2019, he received a President's Medal of Excellence "for intercultural awareness" from UBC, and in October 2023 he was given an honorary Doctor of Laws from

Simon Fraser University for "inspir[ing] countless generations to learn more about Indigenous histories, rights, and relations in Canada, including the history of First Nations and early Chinese migrants." In March 2025 he received a King Charles III Coronation Medal. In the last decade he has participated in more than a dozen conferences on Indigenous subjects, including recent dialogues such as Canada's Truth and Reconciliation process, the UBC apology to residential school survivors (alongside then-UBC president Santa Ono), and Challenging Racism 150. He also still gives regular Musqueam welcomes across Greater Vancouver.

Isn't it time he slowed down? Larry has been asking himself the same question.

"I'm losing my hearing, I've got false teeth, I'm going blind and I'm an old fart," he says. "But I'm still able to walk around and think—no dementia or Alzheimer's, so far. People ten, fifteen years younger than me have bad backs. 'How the hell do you keep going, Larry?' I just do."

His failing eyesight means he has to read everything on his phone or computer in a giant font size; he worked on this book squinting at sixteen-point print-outs, which he covered in elegant cursive comments. It also means he had to give up driving a few years ago. "That's why I'm in such good shape," he says, flexing a bicep. "I'm still walking to Save-On-Foods," at 41st Avenue and Dunbar, eight blocks uphill from his house on the reserve, by the old streetcar stop. UBC sends a chauffeur to drive him to and from the campus every Tuesday during term so he can talk with Indigenous students at the weekly free lunch in the First Nations House of Learning. (All Indigenous students are welcome, no questions asked; the burgers, meat and veggie, are from White Spot.)

Still, he's been thinking a lot about his father and grandfather and the bravery it took for them to leave their homes and come to Canada, alone at such a young age. "My dad had the courage to come from China, and I couldn't go to Prince George or Kitimat, because I didn't know anyone," he says. "They were such brave people, settler migrants looking for a place to better their lives and their family's lives. It's amazing. And I couldn't go to Prince George."

"When I think of my life at fourteen," his dad's age when he emigrated, "with my mother, my grandparents, the whole community . . . in later life I've become emotional thinking about that young man coming to a country so foreign; the language, the culture, the people. All the different ways of each society."

He also wonders, "How did I survive that first year? Why the hell am I the one in the family that's still working with at-risk youth, educating people in our language, still working? How the hell did a premature baby do all that, is still doing all that?"

Growing up cash-poor, Larry was always fixing things, for himself or his neighbours or family. Repairing the vacuum cleaner, updating the electrical in the house, painting the inside and the outside, he can't remember how many times. Other people say, I don't know how to do this; he says, "Just look at it, take it apart, you can fix it." Except he's frustrated now; since his eyes started going nothing is easy anymore.

"Don't be dependent on other people to look after you," Larry says. "If you don't know it, learn it. There's no end to learning, you learn things 'til the day you keel over. I wouldn't know what to do with myself otherwise."

He sees all that work as a sort of payback: "All the knowledge, the history, the community has given you, you have to pass that back. If you don't, your community will die. Many people have not come to grips with that."

When he thinks about all the spiritual knowledge that was handed down to him from his mother and grandparents and aunties, "through stories and things like that," he stresses that none of it actually belongs to *him*. "They're something I use," he says. "And if I don't use them properly I will get hurt. I just hold them, and pass them on."

"Who to?"

"My daughter, my stepdaughter, my grandchildren . . .

". . . To Scott Steedman," he adds with a sly sideways look.

"Who writes them down, so others can read them."

"Yeah, and maybe pass them on too. That's what this book is about."

~~~~~~~~~~

"This pathway goes to the community centre," Larry says. We're walking through a beautiful grove of tall coniferous trees, on a meandering, cedar-chip path. There are workout bars on one side and a wooden children's playground with colourful ropes and climbing logs under the branches on the other. Benches and a wooden picnic table are visible in a grove beyond.

"Nice they kept some old Douglas fir here."

"We did as little cutting as we could," Larry says, "because that was part of the allocation of land, that we would leave a certain number of acres of green space. We couldn't cut all the trees down, because they're too precious." He shakes his head, knowing this is all second growth, the scrawny remnants of a rainforest cathedral clear-cut a century ago to make way for the campus of the fledgling university. "UBC already cut down nearly all the trees, but they made us keep a few."

"This is a lit walkway, at night," he adds. "It is an ancient pathway coming through here, one of the original paths heading down to Spanish Banks."

"Pre-contact?"

"Yeah, pre-contact. These were our hunting grounds, and this was a salmon-bearing stream over here."

A right turn takes us to a viewing area overlooking a stunning new water feature, a little pond encircled with grasses and bullrushes. Swallows dart about, chasing insects on the water's surface, while two pairs of mallards splash with their broods of yellow ducklings on the water's edge. Large silver balls decorated with Musqueam patterns glitter on metal poles, a magic touch that somehow fits.

"This brings you right to the bus stop," says Larry. "It's a natural waterway that feeds into Musqueam Creek, the pathway runs along this side here. The water drains that way." He's pointing to a surprisingly beautiful ditch lined with boulders and colourful vegetation that runs along the boulevard on the far side and drains leləm̓'s rainwater.

A bus drops off a group of schoolchildren, who are chatting away noisily as they walk towards the pond, then slowly quiet down as they lean over the wooden fence and take in the humming, bucolic scene: the fuzzy, big-eyed ducklings paddling in the shallows, the sun reflecting off the silver spheres, the lightning-fast swallows defying gravity as they swoop and bank in tight circles, the salal and ferns a bright green trim at the foot of the dark conifers soaring up behind.

Like the forest grove we've just walked through or the marketing copy on the billboards in front of us, it's artificial, a manicured reimagining of nature tailor-made for the wealthy residents of an upmarket condo development in Canada's most expensive city. And it's been squeezed into a leftover bit of space between a busy road loud with buses and dump trucks and a fast-growing cluster of apartment towers.

And yet . . . it's strangely soothing, a little piece of paradise that calms the soul and transfixes the kids on their school outing, mesmerised by the gentle serenity of this re-creation of a salmon stream from three centuries ago, before the explorers came with their guns and germs in their wooden ships, before Captain Grant arrived with the Royal Engineers or his son Seymour held his great potlatch. Before the gold rush and the smallpox epidemic and the railroad and the waves of immigrants arriving on trains and ships brought chaos and change to this beautiful corner of North America and turned the lives of its Indigenous inhabitants upside down forever.

Larry too is quiet. Does the pond remind him of those fields of reeds by the river when he was growing up, or further back, of Musqueam as it must have been for his grandfather, born before the first white settlers started farming on the banks of the Fraser? Or much further back, of c̓əsnaʔəm, the city before the city, where countless generations of Musqueam ate and hunted and loved where the great muddy river met the sparkling blue waters of the Salish Sea?

"Home on sxʷ məokʷoy̓əm aʔt," he says. "Home on stolen, occupied lands."

Thanks

This book took eight years to come into being, the fruit of an unlikely partnership.

Larry and I started our free-ranging conversations after a chance meeting in 2017. I asked him if he was interested in writing his life story one day. Three years later he asked me if I'd like to read some interviews he'd done earlier and help him turn them into something interesting. Many questions followed, so we started meeting in the spring of 2021, on the reserve and on road trips all over Greater Vancouver, recording the conversations. The result is this book.

For Larry, *Reconciling* is an elaboration of the many land acknowledgments and Musqueam welcomes he gives, primarily to non-Indigenous audiences—a deepening of a conversation he's been having with the wider world for decades, on his journey from not-belonging to belonging. I am the audience, a stand-in for the reader who wants to better understand the Indigenous and Chinese Canadian versions of events.

For me, it's about listening; about understanding Larry's life, and what it means about mine.

For both of us, this is the path to reconciliation.

Larry writes:

I would like to thank my co-teacher Dr. Susan Jane Blake and my student and good friend Dr. Ulrich Teucher, for recording the interviews that were the start of this book, and for graciously returning them to me to use as I wish. Thanks also to my older brother Gordon, for being the best protector I could ask for. To my sister Helen, for always pressing my RCAF Cadet uniform so I could pass inspections. To my younger, baby brother Howard, for convincing me to enroll in the Musqueam First Nations Languages Program so that I might have something to do in my retirement from my trades job to fill the time and get a UBC library card.

To my co-teachers who worked with me teaching each other as we taught the students: Dr. Patricia A. Shaw, Dr. Susan J. Blake, Dr. Suzanne Gessner, Fiona Campbell. And to all the people at UBC who heard parts of my story and encouraged me to write a book.

To Sarah Ling and Alejandro Yoshizawa, for creating the documentary film *All Our Father's Relations*. To all our family and community for the support given to me in the language program.

To my mother, who kept me, a premature baby, alive in the third-world conditions our people were forced to live in on the reserves. A woman who was illiterate but the most intelligent, logical person in my upbringing, passing on life skills and knowledge that have guided me through my life. Teachings that I hope I am able to pass on to my family and others.

To my wife, for putting up with me.

Lastly, to my Chinese grandfather, who brought his son to Canada, and to my father, for having the courage to follow him, and for supporting us in difficult circumstances in the best way he could. If they hadn't, would I even be?

///////////////

Scott writes:

I would like to thank Larry Grant for trusting me with his story. I aimed to tell it in a way that was worthy of all he's been through. I am still learning.

Thanks to the British Columbia Arts Council, who gave me a generous grant and kickstarted the writing. Thanks to Michael Holmes and Jen Sookfong Lee and everyone at ECW Press, for their belief and enthusiasm.

And thanks to my dad, John Alan Steedman, who taught me humility and curiosity and some fine folk songs; and to my mum, Jocelyn Steedman (neé Fraser), who read the first fifty pages and sadly did not live to see this book finished, but encouraged me in her reverence for the first people of Canada and Australia, her two homes.

Thanks also to Leilah Nadir, a wonderful writer, collaborator and wife, who read all the early drafts and savaged them lovingly, pushing me to make them better. I love you Leil.

And finally, thanks to my children, Lucas, Zazie, Sami and Rose, who keep me laughing and wondering and feeling older and younger every day.

Sources

All Our Father's Relations, directed by Alejandro Yoshizawa, produced by Sarah Ling, Jordan Paterson and Alejandro Yoshizawa (Vancouver: Right Relations, 2016).

ċəsnaʔəm: the city before the city, directed by Elle-Máijá Tailfeathers, produced by Elle-Máijá Tailfeathers (Vancouver: Musqueam First Nation, 2017).

Chinatown Through a Wide Lens: The Hidden Photographs of Yucho Chow by Catherine B. Clement, CCHS, Vancouver, 2019.

Indigenous Languages Across Canada, Statistics Canada report, March 23, 2023: https://www12.statcan.gc.ca/census -recensement/2021/as-sa/98-200-X/2021012/98-200-X2021012 -eng.cfm

Language City: The Fight to Preserve Endangered Mother Tongues in New York by Ross Perlin, Atlantic Monthly Press, New York, 2024.

Points of Interest: In Search of the Places, People, and Stories of B.C., A Tyee Anthology, edited by David Beers and andrea bennett, Greystone, Vancouver, 2024.

Relationship-Building on Unceded Lands: An Examination and Assessment of the Musqueam–YVR Sustainability and Friendship Agreement by Jessica Lea Carson, MA thesis, University of British Columbia, 2007.

Saltwater City: An Illustrated History of the Chinese in Vancouver by Paul Yee, 2nd edition, Douglas & McIntyre, Vancouver, 2006.

The Story of Dunbar: Voices of a Vancouver Neighbourhood, edited by Peggy Schofield, Ronsdale Press, Vancouver, 2007.

These Mysterious People: Shaping History and Archaeology in a Northwest Coast Community, by Susan Roy, 2nd edition, McGill-Queens University Press, Montreal, 2016.

"We Do Not Talk About Our History Here": The Department of Indian Affairs, Musqueam–Settler Relations, and Memory in a Vancouver Neighbourhood, by Alexandra Sanya Pleshakov, MA thesis, McGill University, 2003.

The West Beyond the West: A History of British Columbia, by Jean Barman, 3rd edition, University of Toronto Press, Toronto, 2007.

The Authors

LARRY GRANT (sʔəyələq, Hong Lai Hing) is an Elder of the Vancouver Chinese community and the Musqueam Indian Band. He is Elder-in-Residence at the University of British Columbia's First Nations House of Learning and the Justice Institute of BC. An adjunct professor with UBC's Musqueam Language Program within the Institute for Critical Indigenous Studies, he co-teaches the first year hənq̓əminəm̓ language course. He is a Faculty Fellow at St. John's College, and the inaugural Honorary Life Fellow for Green College. For his day job he is manager (interim) of the Musqueam Language and Culture Department. He has participated in more than a dozen conferences on Indigenous subjects, including recent dialogues such as Canada's Truth and Reconciliation process, the UBC apology to residential school survivors (alongside UBC president Santa Ono) and Challenging Racism 150.

In 2019, Larry received a President's Medal from UBC, and in October 2023 he was given an honorary Doctor of Laws from Simon Fraser University. In March 2025 he received a King Charles III Coronation Medal. A member of the Mask Dance Society, he has participated in traditional Musqueam ceremonies since 1946, and still gives regular Musqueam welcomes across Greater Vancouver.

Larry lives with his family on Musqueam Reserve No. 2.

SCOTT STEEDMAN is a senior lecturer in the Simon Fraser University Publishing program and a writer and editor. The books he has edited have sold hundreds of thousands of copies and won many awards: *Visions of British Columbia* won the City of Vancouver Book Award and was shortlisted for a BC Book Prize, and a book he acquired, *Something Fierce* by Carmen Aguirre, won CBC Canada Reads 2012 and was a number one bestseller. He has written more than a dozen books for children and adults, including *Art for War and Peace*, which won the 2015 Benjamin Franklin Award. Born in Ontario and raised in Australia and BC, Scott spent many years in London and Paris and now lives with his family in Vancouver, a short bike ride through the forest from Musqueam Reserve No. 2.

Entertainment. Writing. Culture. ────────────

ECW is a proudly independent, Canadian-owned book publisher. We know great writing can improve people's lives, and we're passionate about sharing original, exciting, and insightful writing across genres.

──────────────────────── **Thanks for reading along!**

We want our books not just to sustain our imaginations, but to help construct a healthier, more just world, and so we've become a certified B Corporation, meaning we meet a high standard of social and environmental responsibility — and we're going to keep aiming higher. We believe books can drive change, but the way we make them can too.

Certified

Corporation

Being a B Corp means that the act of publishing this book should be a force for good — for the planet, for our communities, and for the people who worked to make this book. For example, everyone who worked on this book was paid at least a living wage. You can learn more at the Ontario Living Wage Network.

This book is also available as a Global Certified Accessible™ (GCA) ebook. ECW Press's ebooks are screen reader friendly and are built to meet the needs of those who are unable to read standard print due to blindness, low vision, dyslexia, or a physical disability.

FSC
www.fsc.org
MIX
Paper | Supporting
responsible forestry
FSC® C103567

This book is printed on FSC®-certified paper. It contains recycled materials, and other controlled sources, is processed chlorine free, and is manufactured using biogas energy.

ECW's office is situated on land that was the traditional territory of many nations, including the Wendat, the Anishinaabeg, Haudenosaunee, Chippewa, Métis, and current treaty holders the Mississaugas of the Credit. In the 1880s, the land was developed as part of a growing community around St. Matthew's Anglican and other churches. Starting in the 1950s, our neighbourhood was transformed by immigrants fleeing the Vietnam War and Chinese Canadians dispossessed by the building of Nathan Phillips Square and the subsequent rise in real estate value in other Chinatowns. We are grateful to those who cared for the land before us and are proud to be working amidst this mix of cultures.

ecwpress.com